Nonprofit Finance: A Synthetic Review

Voluntaristics Review

Volumes published in this Brill Research Perspectives title are listed at *brill.com/vrbr*

Nonprofit Finance

A Synthetic Review

By

Thad D. Calabrese

BRILL

LEIDEN | BOSTON

This paperback book edition is simultaneously published as issue 4.5 (2019) of *Voluntaristics Review*, DOI:10.1163/24054933-12340030.

ICSERA is a global infrastructure organization, research-information institute, and umbrella association for voluntaristics (nonprofit, third sector) researcher associations (www.icsera.org). A Florida-based, IRS-501(c) (3) nonprofit 2010+, the International Council of Voluntarism, Civil Society, and Social Economy Researcher Associations officially sponsors *Voluntaristics Review* and the *Palgrave Handbook of Volunteering, Civic Participation, and Nonprofit Associations*.

Library of Congress Control Number: 2020930483

Typeface for the Latin, Greek, and Cyrillic scripts: "Brill". See and download: brill.com/brill-typeface.

ISBN 978-90-04-42870-6 (paperback)
ISBN 978-90-04-42871-3 (e-book)

Contents

Nonprofit Finance: A Synthetic Review

Thad D. Calabrese, PhD
Associate Professor
Robert F. Wagner Graduate School of Public Service
New York University
thad.calabrese@nyu.edu

Abstract

The field of finance is concerned with the management of money and how and where such funds are acquired and used. This article reviews the broad literature on finance related to nonprofit and voluntary organizations, identifies gaps in knowledge, and proposes potential avenues for future researchers. It examines in detail the sources of funds for nonprofit organizations, especially nonprofit agencies—including issues around revenue portfolios and interactions, the uses of these funds—with an emphasis on incentives faced by nonprofit organizations around financial disclosures, the benefits and problems of slack resources and profits, and issues of capital structure in nonprofit organizations.

Keywords

revenues – expenses – margin – profits – capital structure – cost of capital – working capital – operating reserves – debt

Synopsis

The field of finance is concerned with the management of money, and how and where such funds are acquired and used. Whereas finance applied to private for-profit organizations is a highly developed field, finance as applied to voluntary agencies and organizations remains in its developmental stage. This article reviews the broad literature on finance related to nonprofit and voluntary organizations, especially nonprofit agencies, identifies gaps in knowledge, and proposes potential avenues for future researchers. Whereas finance applied to private organizations (businesses) is a highly developed field both theoretically and empirically, finance as applied to voluntary agencies and organizations remains in its developmental stage. Unlike private organizations, voluntary agencies and organizations have a public aspect to them in that operations are significantly subsidized by governments and individuals using tax-advantaged donations, and profits must be retained and not distributed to controlling parties; further, voluntary agencies and organizations may have different objective functions than for-profit organizations. First, definitions and characteristics of organizations in the nonprofit sector are discussed. The nonprofit sector is itself is quite diverse, and the finances of organizations within this sector are also quite varied. What is known about the finances of the sector come largely from administrative data of organizations required to file tax information with the federal government. However, we currently lack financial data about much of the third sector at all (small volunteer associations, for example), and lack data on a common and significant input in volunteer donations.

While finance is concerned with the sources and uses of funds of organizations, these sources and uses fundamentally depend on what the goals of these organizations are. A section of this article then discusses the financial objectives of nonprofit organizations. The literature has discussed profit maximization from some or even all of its activities, perhaps to cross-subsidize unprofitable activities. Relatedly, nonprofit managers might gain utility from providing the nonprofit output but negative utility from commercial activity that is used to support the nonprofit output. A second potential financial objective might be budget maximization, in which gross resources are maximized. Entrepreneurs in these nonprofits may find that they accrue more prestige or personal income as the amount of resources controlled by the organization increases. A third financial objective might be labeled a zero-profit constraint. This goal would indicate that expenses and revenues should be perfectly or closely balanced. A fourth financial objective might be described as net worth accumulation, which suggests any profit accumulation is sought by managers and not necessarily a maximum one. A fifth financial objective is one in which profits, while valued, are traded off for other preferences.

The article then discusses the literature on finding the best or optimal mixture of revenues for a nonprofit organization. In particular, this section examines revenue diversity through the lens of portfolio theory. The discussion then analyzes measurement problems in the literature and attempts to reconcile conflicting empirical findings. Then, revenue interactions are explored. Specifically, the literature that examines whether government funds crowd-in or crowd-out private contributions is analyzed, as is the literature on whether commercial revenues crowd-out voluntary donations. Innovations such as social enterprises, different new legal forms, financial instruments, and donor-advised funds are then detailed.

After the sources of funds, the article turns to the uses of these funds. The analysis focuses on the difficulty in measuring and observing outcomes produced by nonprofits. This leads to the use of proxy measures of efficiency that incentivize certain behaviors, such as cost shifting and misreporting.

Nonprofit slack and profits are analyzed, focusing first on how these concepts differ from for-profit organizations. The literature on whether nonprofits seek profits is reviewed, the importance of operating reserves is discussed, and the difficulties in building such reserves is also a focus. This section also examines the literature on foundations, as well as the literature devoted to determining why these distinct nonprofits distribute what they do and, by implication, save what they do. The literature on the distribution behavior of foundations has many sampling and data concerns, and these are also outlined.

The final section of the literature review examines capital structure in nonprofits. This literature examines the cost of capital in nonprofit firms—that is, the costs of issuing debt or the costs of raising equity (net assets). The literature on nonprofit debt instruments is detailed, with a concentration on the use of tax-exempt bonds. Types of equity are also discussed, with attention paid to endowments. A brief discussion on capital budgeting is also included to conclude this section.

Editor's Introduction (V#4): the Larger Context of *Nonprofit Finance: a Synthetic Review*

Business schools have been teaching the subjects of finance, management, operations research, accounting, marketing, managerial economics, information technology, entrepreneurship, and organizational behavior for decades, and there are many well-developed textbooks for these subjects. The same cannot be said for nonprofit organizations and other voluntaristic enterprises. Some of these fields are better developed than others, but perhaps the least-developed field is nonprofit finance theory. There are many how-to guides on aspects of nonprofit financial management (e.g. Batts, 2017; Finkler, Smith, & Calabrese, 2020; McGlaughlin, 2016; Zietlow et al., 2018), which overlaps with, but is distinct from, nonprofit finance theory. There are also many books on fundraising (for example, Tempel, Seiler, & Burlingame, 2016; Worth, 2015), but to my knowledge no comprehensive textbooks on nonprofit finance. Dennis R. Young and his coauthors partially fill this gap, mostly through edited volumes of commissioned essays on various aspects of nonprofit finance (Seaman & Young, 2018; Young, 2006, 2017), but the present article is the first comprehensive treatment of the subject in a fully integrated treatise by a single author. I congratulate Professor Calabrese for this important work.

Nonprofit finance really is different from traditional finance theory. Though less well studied and understood, the field deserves the same rigorous and systematic study as traditional finance. Briefly, these are some of the factors that differentiate the two:

- Nonprofit organizations can generate and accumulate financial surpluses but are prohibited from distributing this surplus to those in control, the board of directors. This "nondistribution constraint" (Hansmann, 1980) defines an organization as nonprofit.
- Shareholders cannot receive dividends and cannot sell their ownership rights for financial gain. Doing so would violate the nondistribution constraint. Instead, the owners receive "dividends-in-kind" (Wedig, 1994) from irreversible investments called donations.
- There can be no traditional equity shareholders, for shares would not hold value except for the prospect of eventual dividend payments, which are prohibited. The nature of equity is altered, and the rules governing debt vs. equity finance must adjust accordingly.
- Because ownership cannot be transferred for profit, nonprofits are not subject to financially motivated takeover bids (Steinberg, 2015). They can pursue their charitable mission without fearing the market for control, and do not need to invest in costly anti-takeover tactics that reduce their efficiency.
- The fundamental goal of nonprofit organizations is not value maximization. Nonprofit objectives are diverse, including objectives relating to the output mix (for example, James, 1983), provision of private benefits to managers and other stakeholders (for example, Eckel & Steinberg, 1993; Pauly & Redisch, 1973; Tullock, 1966), distributional impacts of services (Smith, 2000; Steinberg & Weisbrod, 2005), accumulation of wealth (Hansmann, 1990), and many other factors (generally, see Steinberg, 2006). Value maximization is sometimes a consequence of pursuing these objectives, but departures from value maximization remain important.
- Nonprofit taxation and regulation are distinct, affecting traditional arbitrage relations and altering incentives for financial behaviors.
- Traditional and nonprofit finance both consider choices regarding multiple revenue streams. Some concerns are common across the two—revenue interactions, stability, transaction costs. But nonprofits have unique concerns stemming from grants and donations and from their variety of objective functions.

The scope of Professor Calabrese's article is vast, but some areas of nonprofit finance are omitted or lightly covered. Here are additional topics arguably within the scope of the field of nonprofit finance:

- *Social investment.* This term encompasses a variety of financial instruments called sris (sustainable and responsible investing) designed to limit personal and institutional investments in companies that engage in socially undesirable activities. The most common sri is a social mutual fund that screens out companies based on some combination of environmental, social, and corporate governance (esg) criteria. Other forms include fixed-income and alternative investments and impact investing (socially conscious portfolio selection). The US Social Investment Forum Foundation (2018) estimated that $12 trillion was invested in assets that explicitly incorporate esg criteria or by investors who file shareholder resolutions on esg issues in 2018, about one-quarter of all US-domiciled assets under management that year. Questions arise regarding the ultimate impact of sri, interactions between sri investment and donations, and the appropriate role of sri funds in endowments and nonprofit reserve funds (for example, Kitzmueller & Shimshack, 2012; Salamon, 2014).

- *Behavioral nonprofit finance.* The behavioral revolution is forcing us to re-examine the underlying assumptions of financial economics (Hirshleifer, 2015). Carefully controlled scientific experiments have revealed many cognitive limitations that lead to predictably irrational behavior, and finance theory is evolving accordingly. The impact of factors like loss aversion, over-confidence, reference-dependent utility, errors of commission vs. omission, misperception of risk, and myopia on charitable giving is an active area of research that is explored in the annual Science of Philanthropy conferences cosponsored by the University of Chicago and the Indiana University Lilly Family School of Philanthropy. A similar effort is needed in the other areas of nonprofit finance.

- *Capital budgeting.* Capital budgeting is the branch of corporate finance that examines long-term investments in new plant and equipment, new products, research and development, and the like. Professor Calabrese touches on this subject without pretending to be comprehensive, and I would like to expand his discussion a little bit. Cost-benefit analysis was developed out of capital budgeting analysis to evaluate public projects by Jules Dupuit (1844). As the technique developed further, the focus included estimating the social welfare costs and benefits of activities that are not properly valued in market equilibrium (if valued at all). Similar issues arise when nonprofit organizations decide which approach to take to best advance their mission—which services, programs, facilities, and delivery methods to offer. Therefore, in Young et al. (2019), we argue that something like cost-benefit analysis should be used for all nonprofit capital-budgeting decisions. However, governments implement a consensus notion of the public good, whereas nonprofits implement various and competing private notions of the public good. This requires a re-evaluation of the fundamental underlying assumptions embedded in governmental cost-benefit analysis. Nonprofit missions do not always respect consumer sovereignty, do not always encompass costs and benefits accruing to each person affected by their capital-budgeting decisions, and do not always value every mutually beneficial activity as desirable. We hope that others will further develop this line of research.

References

Batts, M. E. (2017). *Nonprofit financial oversight: The concise and complete guide for boards and finance committees.* (n.p.): Accountability Press. Self-published via CreateSpace Independent Publishing Platform. Available from https://www.nonprofitcpa.com/nfo/.

Dupuit, J. (1844). De la mesure de l'utilité des travaux publics. [English translation: On the Measurement of the Utility of Public Works]. *Annales des ponts et chaussées, 8,* 332–375.

Eckel, C. C. & Steinberg, R. (1993). Competition, performance, and public policy towards nonprofits. In D. R. Young & D. C. Hammack (Eds.), *Nonprofit organizations in a market economy.* (pp. 57–81). San Francisco, CA: Jossey-Bass Publishers.

Finkler, S. A., Smith, D. L., & Calabrese, T. D. (2020). *Financial management for public, health, and not-for-profit organizations.* Thousand Oaks, CA: CQ Press.

Hansmann, H. B. (1980). The role of nonprofit enterprise. *Yale Law Journal, 89*(5), 835–901.

Hansmann. H. (1990). Why do universities have endowments? *Journal of Legal Studies, 19*(1), 3–42.

Hirshleifer, D. (2015). Behavioral finance. *Annual Review of Financial Economics, 7,* 133–159.

James, E. (1983). How nonprofits grow: A model. *Journal of Policy Analysis and Management, 2,* 350–366.

Kitzmueller, M. & Shimshack, J. (2012). Economic perspectives on corporate social responsibility. *Journal of Economic Literature, 50*(1), 51–84.

McLaughlin, T. A. (2016). *Streetsmart financial basics for nonprofit managers,* 4th edition. Hoboken, NJ: John Wiley and Sons.

Pauly, M. & Redisch, M. (1973). The not-for-profit hospital as a physicians' cooperative. *The American Economic Review, 63*(1), 87–99.

Salamon, L. M. (Ed.) (2014). *New frontiers of philanthropy: A guide to the new tools and actors reshaping global philanthropy and social investing.* New York: Oxford University Press.

Seaman, B. A. & Young, D. R. (2018). *Handbook of research on nonprofit economics and management*, 2nd edition. Northampton, MA: Edward Elgar.

Smith, D. H. (2000). *Grassroots associations.* Thousand Oaks, CA; SAGE.

Steinberg, R. (2006). Economic theories of nonprofit organizations. In W. W. Powell & R. Steinberg (Eds.), *The nonprofit sector: A research handbook*, 2nd edition (pp. 117–139). New Haven, CT: Yale University Press.

Steinberg, R. (2015), What should social finance invest in and with whom?. In A. Nicholls, R. Paton, & J. Emerson (Eds.), *Social finance* (pp. 64–95). Oxford: Oxford University Press.

Steinberg, R. & Weisbrod, B. A. (2005). Nonprofits with distributional objectives: Price discrimination and corner solutions. *Journal of Public Economics, 89*(11–12), 2205–2230.

Tempel, E. R., Seiler, T. L., & Burlingame, D. F. (2016). *Achieving excellence in fundraising.* Hoboken, NJ: John Wiley & Sons.

Tullock, G. (1966). Information without profit. *Public Choice, 1*(1), 141–159.

US Social Investment Forum Foundation (2018). 2018 report on US sustainable, responsible and impact investing trends. Available at https://www.ussif.org//Files/Trends/Trends_onepageroverview_2018.pdf.

Wedig, G. (1994). Risk, leverage, donations and dividends-in-kind: A theory of nonprofit financial behavior. *International Review of Economics and Finance, 3*, 257–278.

Worth, M. J. (2015). *Fundraising: Principles and practice.* Singapore: Sage.

Young, D. R. (Ed.) (2006). *Financing nonprofits: Putting theory into practice.* Lanham, MD: Rowman AltaMira.

Young, D. R. (2017). *Financing nonprofits and other social enterprises: A benefits approach.* Northampton, MA: Edward Elgar.

Young, D. R., Steinberg, R., Emanuele, R., & Simmons, W. O. (2019). *Economics for nonprofit managers and social entrepreneurs.* Northampton, MA: Edward Elgar.

Zietlow, J., Hankin, J. A., Seidner, A., & O'Brien, T. (2018). *Financial management for nonprofit organizations: policies and practices.* Hoboken, NJ: John Wiley & Sons.

Richard Steinberg, PhD
Deputy Editor, Voluntaristics Review
Professor of Economics and the Indiana University Lilly Family School of Philanthropy at IUPUI, Indianapolis, IN, USA

1   Introduction

Regardless of form, all organizations must concern themselves with where resources are derived from during the course of operations, and how these resources are used in fulfilling organizational purpose. Further, whether these resources are sourced and expended for routine operations or periodic investing is an additional matter that all entities address. Broadly speaking, the field of finance is concerned with the management of money, and how and where such funds are acquired and used. The field of finance is distinguished from the field of financial management that focuses on generating financial information for improved managerial and board decision making, which is aimed at realizing the mission of the organization while achieving a stable financial position (Finkler, Smith, & Calabrese, 2020).

This article reviews the broad literature on finance related to nonprofit and voluntary organizations, especially nonprofit agencies, identifies gaps in knowledge, and proposes potential avenues for future researchers. While all nonprofit and voluntary organizations may not exist to maximize profits necessarily, finance remains a core management function of entities in the third sector, and its study continues to be an important area of research. Finance and sustainability remain perennial concerns of nonprofit managers, board members, and leaders of voluntary organizations (for example, see Nonprofit Finance Fund, 2018), and research on the topic addresses familiar (and seemingly constant) concerns of the sector. Further, finance is one avenue in which we can study the objective functions of these organizations (for example, Steinberg, 1986a); inference in this critical area may lend insights and solutions for the concerns of managers and volunteers in the field.

Whereas finance applied to private organizations (businesses) is a highly developed field both theoretically and empirically, finance as applied to voluntary agencies and organizations remains in its developmental stage. Unlike private organizations, voluntary agencies and organizations have a public aspect to them in that operations are significantly subsidized by governments and individuals using tax-advantaged donations, and profits must be retained and not distributed to controlling parties; further, voluntary agencies and organizations may have different objective functions than for-profit organizations. Many of the incentives found to exist in the for-profit corporate finance literature—such as tax minimization, increasing firm value, and profit maximization, among others—seem not to be applicable to voluntary agencies and organizations in general. At the very least, these incentives are not the primary drivers of finance decisions in the third sector.

This review is organized as follows. Common definitions are provided next. Section three describes the heterogeneity of the nonprofit sector in form, mission, and type. These variations are important to understand nonprofit finance in general, and how differences influence the financial functions of these organizations. Further, this section attempts to delineate what commonalities nonprofits have with one another. Having established the unit of analysis, the fourth section outlines the basic financial characteristics of the nonprofit sector, or at least the portion that can be described from available data. The fifth section outlines various theories about what the financial goals of nonprofit organizations might be. The sixth section focuses individually on the sources of funds for nonprofit organizations as well as theoretical considerations about revenue portfolios and revenue interactions—including issues about whether certain revenues crowd-in or crowd-out voluntary contributions. This section also details several innovations in sources of funds for nonprofits, but is not exhaustive. After discussing the sources of funds, the logical next step is detailing how these funds are used. This seventh section emphasizes the incentives faced by nonprofit organizations around financial disclosures supporting the nonprofit advantage (relative to for-profits) of trustworthiness. Whatever is left over from the uses of these funds is discussed next. While this eighth section focuses on working capital, operating reserves, and financial slack, it does so keenly aware that nonprofits are frequently unable to use tools that other organizations (public and for-profit) might be able to rely upon. Hence, this section considers why such routine management tools are oftentimes unused in the nonprofit sector. The ninth section focuses on capital structure—the decision to finance assets with some combination of borrowing and equity determined in part by the organization's cost of capital. Nonprofit equity is different than in other sectors, and many nonprofit organizations are unwilling or unable to borrow money from lenders. Such considerations are included as well. Finally, the conclusion synthesizes the findings of these sections. Along the way, an attempt is made to draw out specific unknowns, in the hope that researchers will continue to develop the field of nonprofit finance.

2   Definitions

To aid the reader's understanding of common terminology used in finance and studies about the third sector, important and relevant terms are defined here first.

Assets—Resources, tangible or intangible, owned by an organization. Assets are a stock variable measured at one point in time.

Balance sheet—A financial statement in which an organization's assets, liabilities, and equity/net assets are reported as of the end of the fiscal year (at one point in time) in accordance with generally accepted accounting principles.

Budget—A formal organizational financial plan of where resources are expected to be earned and used during a fiscal year.

Debt financing—Borrowing money from another individual or organization to acquire an asset.

Endowment—Assets owned by nonprofits intended to generate additional revenue for the organization. There are endowments restricted in perpetuity by a donor (a "true" endowment), endowments restricted for time or purpose by a donor (a "term" endowment), and endowments restricted by a board of directors (a "quasi-endowment").

Equity—Traditionally, ownership or the difference between assets and liabilities. In the nonprofit sector, equity is referred to as net assets.

Expenditures—A payment or disbursement to pay for an obligation or acquire an asset. Expenditures are a flow variable measured over the entire fiscal year.

Expenses—The using of money or resources to provide services or generate revenues. Expenses are a flow variable measured over the entire fiscal year.

Liabilities—Resources owed by an organization to other entities or individuals. Liabilities are a stock variable measured at one point in time.

Net income—The difference between revenues and expenses. If positive, net income is frequently called profit or surplus; if negative, net income is frequently called deficit or loss. In the nonprofit sector, net income is called change in net assets. Net income is a flow variable measured over the entire fiscal year.

Nondistribution constraint—The prohibition of distributing profits to controlling parties such as boards of directors or other controlling parties. The nondistribution constraint distinguishes nonprofits from for-profit entities.

Operating reserves—Liquid assets maintained by organizations for use to pay for unexpected expenses or to compensate for revenues that do not materialize as expected.

Operating statement—A financial statement in which an organization's revenues, expenses, and profit or loss for the year are reported according to generally accepted accounting principles. Also called an income statement, a profit and loss statement, a statement of revenues and expenses, and an activity statement, the operating statement is a flow statement.

Overhead spending—Generally speaking, overhead spending includes expenses classified as fundraising, management, and general.

Revenues—Money that an organization has either received or is entitled to receive in exchange for providing goods or services. Revenues are a flow variable measured over a fiscal year.

Support—In the nonprofit sector, money that is received or promised in the form of contributions or grants; these revenues are given voluntarily and no exchange of goods or services occurs. Support and the term donations are essentially synonymous.

Taxable debt financing—A form of borrowing in which the interest received by investors is included as part of personal income in calculating tax liability.

Tax-exempt debt—A form of borrowing in which the interest received by investors is excluded from personal income in calculating tax liability. Because the income is tax-exempt, investors are generally willing to accept lower yields on the debt, so the issuers pay less interest as a result compared to taxable debt.

Working capital—The liquid assets that an organization maintains to pay for liabilities due in the near future.

3   Types and Numbers of Nonprofits

Before delving into the finances of nonprofits and what the literature describes and predicts, it is worthwhile to define what is meant by "nonprofit." Indeed, the sector is a diverse amalgamation of very distinct entities with distinctive financial characteristics and legal reporting requirements. Smith (2017) describes three types of nonprofit entities that each have distinct differentiating characteristics. The first is "voluntary associations," in which participating members elect governing agents and exercise a "bottom-up" or democratic organizational form (Smith, 2015). Frequently, these voluntary associations have no paid staff, very small budgets derived primarily from their membership (frequently in the form of dues), and most of the benefits are targeted to these members. This type of nonprofit organization is distinct from "nonprofit agencies," which tend to have self-perpetuating boards, paid staff, larger budgets, benefits targeted to stakeholders outside the organization, and revenues derived from funders, donors, exchange transactions, or other sources consistent with its mission. The third type of nonprofit organization are "foundations." These special types of nonprofits exist to provide grants to other (mostly) nonprofit organizations, tend to have governing bodies that are self-perpetuating, may or may not have paid staff, and target benefits outside the foundation. However, some foundations do exist to provide support to a single related nonprofit, such as a college or a university.

In addition to Smith's (2017) distinctions, some nonprofits have boards appointed by external parties—for example, elected governors may appoint board members for the operating foundations for state universities. Still other nonprofits have characteristics that mix the categories above. Rather than strict legal categories, this description is intended only to highlight the heterogeneity of what scholars and the public refer to as "nonprofit organizations."

In the United States, there are approximately 1.6 million nonprofit organizations registered with the Internal Revenue Service (IRS) (McKeever, 2018). However, organizations that are religious, auxiliaries of these religious organizations, and entities with gross receipts normally less than $5,000 annually are tax exempt.[1] Grønbjerg, Liu, and Pollak (2010) find that more than three-quarters of surveyed nonprofits (those incorporated in Indiana but not registered with the IRS) fell into these statutory omission categories. Given the reality that most voluntary associations fall below this threshold, the true number of exempt organizations in the US is unknown but assumed to be several multiples of the officially registered number. For example, Smith (2000) estimates that informal, volunteer-operated grassroots organizations are likely to be five to ten times as numerous as formal (and, by implication, registered) nonprofits, and Smith (1997) estimates that IRS filings fail to capture 90 percent of nonprofit organizations. Grønbjerg and Clerkin (2005) find registrations of nonprofit organizations are higher when using state registries rather than relying only upon the federal one.

In the US, the tax code delineates the types of organizations that are exempt from taxation. 26 U.S.C. § 501(c) lists twenty-nine different types of organizations that are exempt from federal income taxes. Subsection 3 contains many of the corporations individuals think of when they hear the term "nonprofit," as these 501(c)3 organizations are operated exclusively for charitable purposes and are largely the "nonprofit agencies" described by Smith (2015). In the US, these charitable organizations include hospitals, universities, private secondary schools, and museums, organizations that oftentimes project the trappings of the for-profit sector (for example, high managerial salaries, large investments

---

1 See Internal Revenue Service, "Application for Recognition of Exemption" available at: https://www.irs.gov/charities-non-profits/application-for-recognition-of-exemption.

in fixed assets, generous benefits for top employees, among others). 501(c)4 organizations include many social welfare organizations that operate for the public benefit. Examples of these organizations include volunteer fire companies, homeowners and community associations, and community sports leagues, among others. These organizations include many of the organizations described as "nonprofit associations."

The IRS annually publishes data on federally registered exempt organizations that must file tax information in the Exempt Organization Business Master File (EO BMF).[2] Based on 2018 filings, approximately 77 percent of filers are these 501(c)3 charities, while the remainder are various social welfare organizations, civic leagues, business leagues, labor organizations, etc. Again, these data do not include associations that are not registered with the federal government and exclude organizations that do not meet the minimum receipts needed to require filings. All private foundations (both operating and non-operating)[3] in the US are required to file annual Form 990-PF, and nonprofit agencies with $50,000 in annual gross receipts are required to file a Form 990 or 990-EZ. Prior to 2010, this threshold was $25,000 of gross annual receipts. Organizations that fail to reach the required threshold for filing are expected to file an annual Form 990-N, which is a postcard that indicates the registered nonprofit is still in operation.

Salamon, Sokolowski, and Geller (2012) estimate nonprofit employment at approximately 10 percent of the total private paid workforce; given current levels of private employment, this would suggest that there are 12–13 million employees in the US nonprofit sector.[4] Others, such as McKeever, Dietz, and Fyffe (2016), find slightly higher levels of employment in the US nonprofit sector—perhaps as many as 15 million employees. Internationally, the nonprofit sector is estimated to employ 7.4 percent of the workforce on average (Salamon et al., 2013); extrapolating this to the world labor force results in a nonprofit labor force of over 250 million workers.[5] All these estimates point to a large and important third sector across much of the globe.

However, these estimates fail to capture volunteer labor, which dwarfs paid employment. In the US, more than one-quarter of the population, or nearly 64 million individuals, reported volunteering with an organization in 2016,

---

2 Available from: https://www.irs.gov/charities-non-profits/exempt-organizations-business -master-file-extract-eo-bmf.

3 Private operating foundations use investment income to fund charitable programs that it operates itself. Non-operating foundations grant money to other organizations to provide charitable programs.

4 Derived from data found at: https://fred.stlouisfed.org/series/USPRIV.

5 Worldwide labor force data found at: https://data.worldbank.org/indicator/sl.tlf.totl.in.

and if counted as full-time equivalents would add more than 5 million workers to the nonprofit labor force.[6] Therefore, the number of volunteers was much larger than paid workers, and including them would increase the nonprofit labor force numbers by 40–50 percent.

Salamon, Sokolowski, and Haddock (2011) note that the lack of systematic comparative data focusing on volunteering has significant consequences for our study of nonprofit organizations. For purposes here, the lack of data limits visibility on volunteering. When something is opaque or invisible, it is difficult to study. In the case of nonprofit finance, volunteering represents a significant sector-wide input for generating organizational outputs, and yet the data on the recipient organizational level about volunteering scarcely exist for analysis. In the US, generally accepted accounting principles (GAAP) limit the recording of volunteer time in the financial statements of nonprofit organizations. Currently, only donated services that require specialized skills, are provided by individuals with those specialized skills, and would typically be purchased absent the volunteered time are recognized as a financial event in the financial statements (FASB, 1993). The Form 990 that tax-exempt entities file with the IRS also excludes volunteer labor, although such donated services may be noted outside of the required financial disclosures. Hence, while nonprofits record and report contributions that are cash or pledges to contribute in the future, the current reporting regime does not report most donations of labor which may be a key source of inputs for the third sector. This acknowledgment is significant and is a limitation in our understanding of nonprofit finance.

The point of this discussion is two-fold. Firstly, the generic term "nonprofit" masks great variation in organizational form, governance, and function. By extension, the finances of these different types of group are also unclear as a result. Secondly, what we do know about nonprofits is largely the result of the data we do have, and these data do not include information on those organizations who most populate the sector. Further, these organizations excluded from most data tend to be those nonprofits with the most volunteers. In some sense, nonprofit finance research frequently uses the data available simply because it is all that is available, not because it is the data that researchers actually *need*. In fact, we currently lack financial data about much of the third sector at all (small volunteer associations, for example), and lack data on a common and significant input in volunteer donations.

---

6 Data obtained from: https://nccs.urban.org/data/nonprofit-sector-brief-volunteering-data#.

4   Basic Financial Characteristics of Nonprofit Organizations

This section outlines basic descriptive financial information about the non-profit sector. The intent is to provide an overview of size and scope of resources owned and available in the sector. In a sixteen-country study, Salamon et al. (2013) find that nonprofit organizations contribute between 1 and almost 9 percent of national GDP, with an average contribution of 4.5 percent of GDP. Great variation exists between countries: Thailand's nonprofits contribute 1.6 percent, while Canada's contribute 8.1 percent of GDP. These figures include estimated volunteering time.

Using the National Center for Charitable Statistics (NCCS) Core files for 2015, we can observe a portion of the nonprofit sector's finances. As noted, however, the data do not include the economic value of volunteer labor, which are argu-ably the most important income source to many small voluntary associations. Further, the Core files focus only on 501(c)3 public charities. Nevertheless, in 2015 the mean income for registered and reporting nonprofit organizations was just over $3.1 million; however, the skew within this sample is quite large. The median income was $112,000, and the reported income at the 75th percen-tile is about $373,000. Total income at the 95th percentile is nearly $5.2 million. The data indicate a concentration of total income in the top few percentiles of the sector.

Total assets at the end of 2015 for this sample averaged just under $9.3 mil-lion. As with income, the skewness is significant. The median asset value was $166,000, and total assets for the organization at the 90th percentile was just under $3.3 million, which is still below the mean for the group. Like income, total assets are concentrated in the top percentiles of the sector. These income and wealth concentrations do not appear to be a uniquely American phe-nomenon; Smith (2014) notes a similar pattern in the UK, Australia, Canada, and Israel.

The remainder of this article focuses on five topics that represent some of the most important threads of the nonprofit finance literature.

5   What are the Financial Goals of Nonprofit Organizations?

While finance is concerned with the sources and uses of organizations' funds, these sources and uses fundamentally depend on what the goals of these organizations are. Here, we first consider the objectives of the nonprofit orga-nization in general, and then discuss the financial objectives that emerge from this literature on general organizational objectives.

5.1   *Nonprofit Objectives*

Young (1981) argues that the objectives of a nonprofit organization are themselves derived from the objectives of the entrepreneur who establishes its culture and inculcates it within the governance structure of the organization (through, for example, bylaws). Steinberg (2006) catalogs various objectives that an entrepreneur (defined as a founder or a change agent for an existing nonprofit) might consider, and whether these objectives might be accomplished through the nonprofit form.[7] Entrepreneurs may wish to ensure that collective goods are available, either because they themselves are consumers of the good or because they gain personal fulfillment from providing them to the public. A second type of organizational objective involves altering others' preferences or consumption. This might be related to art, faith or religion, or other activities that change social behavior or interactions. A third category of objective focuses on establishing and maintaining trust between the organization and consumers and donors. A fourth category is about affecting the distribution of income, while a fifth type of objective is income derived as well as perquisites. These perquisites might include the warm glow from doing good, but can also include any compensation that is nonmonetary—such as reputational enhancement, travel benefits, etc. The final category consists of private benefits not captured by other categories. These include "power, control, expression, affiliation, legitimation, and the like" (Steinberg, 2006, p. 131). Steinberg (2006) notes that many existing models of nonprofit behavior assume mixed motives—for example, quantity and quality of outputs might be conceived as providing public goods while maintaining public trustworthiness potentially. In addition, other entrepreneurs will be constrained to pursue different objectives than what they truly want. Nevertheless, this brief summary of organizational objectives based on the objectives of entrepreneurs is highlighted so that we can discuss the financial objectives that emerge organically from this literature.

5.2   *Nonprofit Financial Objectives*

Just as numerous as the objectives of entrepreneurs, the current literature has considered at least five different financial objectives for nonprofits. Firstly, nonprofits might seek profit maximization from some or even all of its activities. Doing so ensures money exists to meet whatever the ultimate goal(s) of the entrepreneur and organization is or are. This notion can be extended to

---

7   Readers interested in these objectives and the sources from which his model derive should consult this chapter.

cross-subsidization, in which profitable activities support unprofitable activities. James (1983) notes that the more nonprofit organizations "wish to carry out loss-making activities, the more they seek out profitable activities to provide them with the necessary resources" (p. 352). Because nonprofits are "consumption-oriented" organizations, there is a perpetual need for resources. Hence, profits from these profitable activities ("production activities") will be maximized to cross-subsidize activities that are mission-critical but lose money ("consumption activities").

Schiff and Weisbrod (1991) expand upon this theme and hypothesize that the nonprofit manager gains utility from providing the nonprofit output but negative utility from commercial activity that is used to support the nonprofit output. Schiff and Weisbrod (1991) also point out that as nonprofit output losses grow, commercial activity increasingly subsidizes the output; however, this makes the sector less desirable for nonprofit entrepreneurs. This might suggest that profit maximization per se is not the goal of commercial activity, but the maximum amount that still permits ample utility derivation from the nonprofit output. Similarly, Eckel and Steinberg (1993) find profit maximization from commercial activity subsidizes private-benefit managerial perks and also public-benefit perks. Profits from high-end consumers may subsidize the prices to low-end consumers and increase social welfare overall (Steinberg & Weisbrod, 1998). Overall, while there are certainly examples or subsectors of nonprofits that exhibit profit-maximizing behavior, Weisbrod (1998) details how such seemingly uncharitable behavior might actually benefit the mission orientation of nonprofits. In contrast, using a very unique cooperative market of the nonprofit hospital as the unit of analysis, Pauly and Redisch (1973) model profit maximization from commercial activity; the goal of this profit maximization, however, is not to cross-subsidize charitable output, but instead to maximize the per member physicians' net incomes. Preston (1988) further notes that the assumption that nonprofits derive utility from generating social benefits is not sensible in competitive mixed industries. These results might suggest that profit maximization for cross-subsidization is not a universal objective, perhaps limited to those nonprofits not operating in mixed industries.

A second potential financial objective might be budget maximization, in which gross resources are maximized (Steinberg, 1986). Both Tullock (1966) and Niskanen (1971) speculate that some nonprofits will set this as a goal; similar to the public choice model in economics, entrepreneurs in these nonprofits may find that they accrue more prestige or personal income as the amount of resources controlled by the organization increases. Steinberg (1986) also notes that self-dealing might be more lucrative in larger organizations in general, and the nonprofit sector is not exempt from this reality. In a survey of religious nonprofit organizations, Zietlow (1989) finds donation (revenue) maximization the chief financial goal of nearly one-third of respondents, suggesting that budget maximization is not limited to secular nonprofits. Zietlow (1989) speculates that increased revenues lead to increased spending on charitable outputs or quality that benefits the nonprofit.

A third financial objective might be labeled a zero-profit constraint. This goal would indicate that expenses and revenues should be perfectly or closely balanced. Because of the nondistribution constraint, some literature has modeled nonprofit behavior as having such a breakeven constraint (see, for example, Freeman, 1979; Scanlon, 1980). Relatedly, in an examination of hospitals, Newhouse (1970) theorized organizations have a goal to maximize outputs subject to a balanced budget constraint (that is, without profits). To this point about zero profits, breakeven financial goals were reported by 45 percent of respondents in Zietlow's (1989) survey of religious nonprofit organizations. The underlying assumption of this objective is that profits serve no management or organizational goal.

A fourth financial objective might be described as net worth accumulation. The reality that nonprofits report net assets in excess of $0 (meaning, they had earned more revenues than they had used over time) suggested to Tuckman and Chang (1992) different goals. Hansmann (1987) and Tuckman (1993) point out that nonprofit financing sources are more limited than sources for other for-profit firms. Some (such as Calabrese, 2012) have suggested that organizations may seek to accumulate these resources over time to generate needed capital. Alternately, these profits might exist simply to prevent financial distress. This objective is different from profit maximization, however, because it suggests any profit accumulation is sought by managers but not necessarily a maximum one.

A fifth financial objective is one in which profits, while valued, are traded off for other preferences. This is not to suggest that the value of profits is driven to zero, but that service quality (as but one example) is at least as important. Rose-Ackerman (1986) describes nonprofit managers concerned with financial health but willing to trade it off for other preferences. In some sense, this is an extension from James (1983), but simply relaxes the assumption that the trade-off is for another unprofitable service and permits virtually any preference to stand. Like net worth accumulation, this objective understands the value of profits but also that other activities or preferences are just as valuable. Chang and Tuckman (1990), for example, suggested that profits could be used to reduce prices for clients or to become independent from donor expectations.

While the literature has not converged necessarily upon an agreed upon financial objective of all nonprofits (perhaps an unrealistic and unattainable result given the heterogeneity of the sector), the notion that profits—whether maximized or just targeted—are unimportant to organizations no longer seems plausible. At the very least, empirical evidence does suggest that profits earned by nonprofits are used to cross-subsidize unprofitable activities; further, organizations do appear to accumulate profits over time, but these profits are not simply masking for-profits operating as nonprofits within the sector.

6   Sources of Funds

6.1   *Overview*
This section offers an overview of revenue sources for nonprofit organizations, and also provides descriptive details on the major revenue sources for the non-profit sector. In describing these various revenue sources individually, relevant literature is also discussed.

501(c)3 public charities registered with the IRS reported nearly $2 trillion in total revenues in 2016.[8] However, this does not include those nonprofits or voluntary associations not required to file with the IRS, usually because of insufficient reported revenues. Recent data indicate that only about 34 percent of registered nonprofit agencies or foundations were required to file annual tax information with the IRS (McKeever, 2018). In 2010, all registered nonprofits reported just under $2.1 billion in total revenues, and just over $1.6 billion in 2005. Since 2005, total nonprofit revenues have grown over 20 percent on an inflation-adjusted basis. These numbers do not include most volunteer labor.

6.2   *Summary of Individual Revenue Sources*
This section describes the major individual revenue sources for nonprofit organizations. This is not an exhaustive list of nonprofit revenue sources and is instead limited to the largest and most significant. Before discussing the major individual revenue sources and appropriate literature about them, a brief discussion about nonprofit financial data sources is included.

6.2.1   Data
What we know about different revenue sources for nonprofit organizations is generally fraught with data limitations. In the US, the Form 990 serves as

8   Based on McKeever (2018).

the primary data source for researchers, and comparable sources exist in some other countries as well.[9] In the US, the Form 990 is not an audited financial statement, and is instead a tax information return. Federal government oversight of the nonprofit sector—which is exempt from corporate income taxation—is managed by the federal tax collector. The Form 990 is most concerned, therefore, with nonprofit agencies' revenues that might be subject to taxation, such as unrelated business income—that is, income earned that is not associated with the organization's charitable mission.

Nonprofit agencies are required to make their Form 990s available to the public. The IRS, as well as private entities, such as the NCCS at the Urban Institute and Guidestar, make data from filed Form 990s available to the public. Different files contain different samples of nonprofit agencies as well as different levels of data derived from the Form 990. The business master files (BMF) are released by the IRS to the public several times each year. The BMF files contain data on all organizations registered with the IRS as exempt entities. They are, therefore, comprehensive with respect to organizations that are registered and file routinely with the IRS. However, the BMF files contain very few of the financial variables of interest for scholars. For example, while the BMF files contain variables for total revenues in a given fiscal year, the individual sources of revenue are not provided. Similarly, while researchers can observe the total assets of nonprofit agencies, the various types of assets are unavailable in the BMF.

The NCCS also produces and makes available a Core file which is composed of active nonprofit organizations (agencies, foundations, and other exempt organizations) that have filed a Form 990 within a particular year. Unlike the BMF, which tends to be released with regularity, the Core files tend to lag by several years; for example, at the beginning of 2019, Core data from 2015 are available (although incomplete). This lag results from some data verification by the NCCS as well as routine lags in reporting by nonprofit entities themselves. In the past, the Core files contained limited financial fields but a much more expansive amount compared to the BMF files. The Core files did provide additional details on some sources of revenues, some uses of funds, and types of liabilities for example, but the data did not provide details on types of assets, all revenue sources reported on the income statement, or the breakdown of net assets by donor restrictions, among others. Beginning in 2012, the amount

---

9 As but one example, registered charities in Canada must file a T3010 Registered Charity Information Return. Similar to US nonprofit agencies, the data are limited to registered organizations and do not include small or unregistered voluntary associations.

of financial detail was expanded to include virtually all the available balance sheet and income statement variables.

The IRS also publishes the Statistics of Income Exempt Organizations Samples File (SOI). The data are a weighted sample of the organizations that file the Form 990, and represent the largest (based on assets) organizations in the sector. Hence, while it may not be comprehensive in terms of number of organizations included, it does capture the majority of sector-wide assets and revenues. The IRS verifies data before releasing, which results in a lag in data reaching researchers. For example, at the beginning of 2019, the IRS had posted SOI data through 2015 on its website.[10] The SOI data contain the most detailed number of variables on balance sheet and income statement variables, but does not contain information on which nonprofit subsector the organization belongs to.

The discussion about available data is intended to highlight an unfortunate reality about nonprofit finance research in general. Researchers are limited to databases they can use depending upon the research question they are pursuing. A researcher investigating capital structure, for example, might find only the SOI data containing the fields necessary for model testing; but the SOI data might limit the generalizability of the empirical findings. Alternatively, the researcher might choose to enhance generalizability by using the Core files, but have to operationalize key constructs suboptimally due to the limited data fields available. The research trade-offs are real and ought to be acknowledged without preventing knowledge building in this area.

Recently, the Form 990s filed electronically have been made available to researchers (see, for example, Lecy, 2019). While electronic filing is currently voluntary, recent federal legislation (the Taxpayers First Act of 2019) mandated electronic filing for all nonprofits required to file the Form 990. While the current sample of electronic filers is nonrandom because of the voluntary nature of electronic filing, this will be less of a concern going forward when all organizations are filing in the same manner. Further, these electronic data contain all the variables available on the Form 990.

6.2.2 Voluntary Contributions

Even in the presence of significant limitations, the Form 990 does inform our understanding of nonprofit agencies' sources of revenues. Nonprofit agencies tend to report multiple sources of funds; Chang and Tuckman (1994) note, for example, that 95 percent of nonprofits report multiple income sources on the

---

10   https://www.irs.gov/statistics/soi-tax-stats-charities-and-other-tax-exempt-organiza
      tions-statistics.

Form 990. Voluntary donations represent a significant and important revenue source for many nonprofit organizations. In 2017, $410 billion (2.1 percent of US GDP) was donated to charitable nonprofit agencies.[11] More than 70 percent of this giving comes from living individuals, about 16 percent from foundations, 5 percent from corporations, and the remainder comes from miscellaneous sources such as bequests. The source of most of these philanthropic dollars in the US, therefore, is not from large institutions, but rather from individual households. Different subsectors within the US nonprofit agency industry receive different amounts of these voluntary donations. For example, nearly one-third of the donations went to religious organizations—typically to houses of worship that individuals belong to—while only 3 percent of donations went to nonprofit agencies focused on the environment.[12] Nonprofit hospitals tend to receive very little in terms of voluntary donations, while colleges and universities typically receive a small but still significant amount of donations annually (especially from alumni). Organizations not required to file informational returns may earn revenues from different sources than organizations that must file. It is likely that most sources of funds are in the form of donated labor and voluntary contributions.

Weisbrod (1975) posits that nonprofits supplement governmental provision of public goods to meet the desires of individuals who have demand for public goods that exceed the demand of the median voter. Nonprofits are supported in part because of this excess demand, and high public good demanders are expected to provide contributions (of time and money) to these nonprofits. Collective action through the nonprofit resolves the under-provision of public goods by the public sector. Others who did not contribute could enjoy these public goods, resulting in a free-rider problem. Fundamentally, this is the problem with donations—there are not enough because some will not donate despite receiving the benefits. Weisbrod's (1975) theory fundamentally seeks to explain why voluntary contributions to nonprofits exist despite this free-rider problem.

Building on ideas from Becker (1974) and Arrow (1974) that charitable behavior is not always induced by altruism, Andreoni (1990) argues that donors gain utility from increasing the supply of privately provided public goods through their donation but also gain utility from the very act of giving. This impure altruism suggests that individuals do care about who donates and that individuals are not indifferent to donations made by others or the government

---

11   This and all donation data from *Giving USA 2018, the Annual Report on Philanthropy*, available at: https://www.charitynavigator.org/index.cfm?bay=content.view&cpid=42.

12   Ibid.

(because these gifts by others do not increase the utility of the donor). Steinberg (1987) extends the impure altruism approach to cases where the public good provided by government and other donors is an imperfect substitute or even complement to the public good provided by the act of giving. Thus, giving results in a private benefit to the donor—such as recognition, premier seats (at a cultural event, for example), reduction in social pressures to contribute, the reward from the act of giving itself (similar to Arrow, 1974), or some other feeling of satisfaction. Such impure altruism does not undermine Weisbrod's (1975) theory, but rather aligns it with reality more fully. Recent advances in experiments and natural analyses continue to find support for the free-rider problem, although the problem is less serious than originally believed (see, for example, Andreoni, Harbaugh, & Vesterlund, 2008, and Vesterlund, 2016, for surveys detailing these studies).

Many nonprofit agencies rely upon donations solicited from donors in traditional forms: telemarketing campaigns, mass mailings, events, and donations from board members. James (2018) notes that noncash gifts to nonprofits, a relatively overlooked reality in much of the research, seem to correlate with future contribution growth. Incorporating donations of financial assets (such as stocks or bonds) or nonfinancial assets (such as property) into future analyses focused on donations might yield fruitful results. Further, nonprofits have moved towards new fundraising innovations as well to reach more and different types of donors. Crowdsourcing, for example, is a means by which nonprofits have secured funding from online users or communities. Frequently, nonprofits might recognize these donors with a prominent acknowledgment on the organization's website (Saxton, Oh, & Kishore, 2013), not unlike the prominent displays of benefactors' names on nonprofits' brick and mortar properties secured via philanthropic support. For nonprofit entrepreneurial projects, perceived risk and the gender of the entrepreneur seem important for success, while humanitarian project funding success is frequently the result of funders' physical proximity to the project (Moleskis, Alegre, & Canela, 2019). The point here is to simply note that the nonprofit sector continues to cultivate existing revenue sources using new technology that hopefully connects the sector with new and different generations of givers. What we know about the effectiveness of these efforts, however, is very limited—partially because the topic is relatively new and partially due to the lack of data.

6.2.3   Program Service Revenues

Based on Tinkelman and Neely (2018), nearly three-quarters of nonprofit revenues are earned from program services. The majority of sector-wide revenues, thus, are derived from providing services to clients or customers and receiving some form of payment. Frequently for nonprofit agencies, clients or customers may not directly pay for the service consumed. For example, third-party insurance companies (private and public) frequently pay for the services consumed by patients in nonprofit health care organizations; governments provide significant resources to pay for costs in higher education for certain students; parents of students pay for tuition costs in private nonprofit secondary schools; and so on.

Program service revenue provides obvious benefits to nonprofits. Many nonprofits provide private goods that are excludable and rival (Chang & Tuckman, 1996), and charging for these services is logical. Further, James (1983) and Weisbrod (1998) model nonprofits as multiproduct organizations, in which mission-oriented programs that lose money may be subsidized by earned-income areas. Cross-subsidization in this case essentially requires commercial income. The downside to program revenue includes mission drift (James & Young, 2007), in which the nonprofit moves toward increasingly commercial activity and away from its core mission programs. Further, Oster (1995) suggests that in addition to mission drift, such commercial ventures may potentially not contribute much to mission. Managers with successful ventures might opt to focus more attention on the business rather than soliciting donations.

6.2.4   Investment Income

Investment income consists primarily of interest, dividends, and capital gains. Investment income can augment nonprofit spending without the organization incurring many of the costs associated with fundraising. Because of this independence from fundraising, many nonprofits seek to own assets significant enough to generate investment earnings that can be used for programmatic purposes. Further, Hansmann (1990) raises concerns that investment income is not expended on mission services and is instead being retained; and indeed one potential downside to investment income is that the nonprofit, like for earned income, will focus more on managing its investment portfolio and spend less time devoted to mission activities. Similarly, Chang and Tuckman (1990) posit that nonprofit managers are motivated by this accumulation of surplus funds rather than devoting them to mission. Because programs rarely have claims on investment income, this becomes a prime source of problematic nonprofit hoarding behavior.

6.2.5   Benefits Theory, or Why Nonprofits Seek Different Revenue Sources

Distinct from various theories or research on individual revenue sources, Young (2007, 2017) offers a "benefits theory" for why nonprofits may pursue different revenues. Rather than nonprofits choosing revenue streams for risk and reward reasons, the benefits theory suggests that these revenues instead are (or should be) reflective of the organization's mission. Organizational activities benefit particular constituents, and revenues should reflect who benefits from the services. For example, benefits that accrue to the public at large (such as a vaccine program) should be financed by the public at large (through tax-advantaged private philanthropy or government) while benefits that accrue to private entities (such as particular medical interventions) should be financed via user fees. In fact, Fischer, Wilsker, and Young (2010) find that nonprofit agencies engaging in services largely providing private benefits earn more income from program service revenues (from fees and charges), and those engaging in services largely providing public benefits earn more income from charitable contributions. They also found heterogeneity of revenue sources between nonprofit subsectors based on these differences in benefits. Organizations with mixed outputs—some benefiting the public and some benefiting private entities—displayed more diversified revenues than those with concentrated benefits. Wilsker and Young (2010) find similar results—that spending benefiting private parties relies upon earned income while spending benefiting public parties relies upon philanthropy—in a subsequent analysis. Benefits theory, therefore, suggests that revenue sources are linked closely with organizational mission—making an explicit connection between nonprofit finance and organizational purpose. The theory also may help guide individual nonprofits in determining which particular type of revenues might be appropriate for diversification purposes; or which ones might be appropriate to concentrate on.

6.2.6   Within-Sector Differences

The discussion above masks another important characteristic in nonprofit finance research—namely that different subsectors of organizations report reliance upon different types of revenues. Differences are briefly examined here using the NCCS Core files for 2015. Given the data limitations of the file, revenues reported as "Contributions" include donations from individuals, fundraising events, special events, federated campaigns, and government grants; "Investment Income" includes dividends, interest, and the income derived from the investment of tax-exempt bond proceeds; "Earned Income" includes program service revenues, net rental income, royalties, and the sale of other assets; and "Other Income" is a catch-all for the remaining revenues that are not reported in these other categories. The reported subsectors are derived from the National Taxonomy of Exempt Entities (NTEE) used by the IRS to classify nonprofit organizations.

TABLE 1   Average source of total revenues for nonprofit agencies for 2015, by subsector

	Contributions	Investment income	Earned income	Other income
Arts, culture, and humanities	27.2% (37.3%)	4.4% (16.7%)	63.0% (39.7%)	5.3% (16.6%)
Education	20.1% (35.4%)	3.3% (14.7%)	73.4% (38.2%)	3.1% (12.4%)
Health	20.3% (34.0%)	4.7% (16.6%)	71.6% (37.0%)	3.4% (12.4%)
Human services	26.3% (37.5%)	2.7% (11.8%)	64.9% (39.8%)	6.0% (16.9%)
Other	30.7% (36.9%)	5.8% (18.6%)	57.8% (38.9%)	5.2% (15.9%)
Total	28.0% (37.0%)	4.5% (16.2%)	62.0% (39.4%)	5.2% (15.9%)

SOURCE: AUTHOR'S CALCULATIONS. DERIVED FROM NCCS CORE 2015 DATA FILES.
ROWS MAY NOT SUM TO 100% DUE TO ROUNDING. PERCENTAGES IN PARENTHESES
ARE STANDARD DEVIATIONS.

The Table 1 summary of nonprofit agencies' revenue sources illustrates not only the significant dependence on average on earned-income streams, but the variation of revenue stream dependence between subsectors. Education and health agencies report higher percentages of income earned from exchange transactions, while other nonprofit agencies report greater revenue portfolios derived from voluntary contributions.

   Within each of these subsectors, significant variation exists as well, and are represented with the reported standard deviations (in the parentheses)—a fairly common statistic of variation or dispersion. Table 1 shows that within each subsector (as well as the sector taken together as a whole), there are many individual organizations far above and below the reported mean values. Therefore, the averages presented in Table 1 are illustrative but perhaps not representative of many individual organizations because of the wide dispersion of values. Overall, Table 1 describes a sector that relies upon several revenue sources to provide goods and services, and that significant variation exists not only between subsectors but even within these subsectors. Describing an "average nonprofit agency," therefore, is difficult.

6.3   Revenue Diversity

All organizations, regardless of mission, require financial resources to pay for routine operations.[13] This section focuses on literature about finding the best or optimal mixture of revenues for a nonprofit organization. Kingma (1993) focuses on a critical theme in the revenue diversity literature—the importance of financial predictability, which he defines as the ability to predict annual changes in organizational revenues relatively accurately. Fundamentally, "unpredictability [of revenues] has a real cost that nonprofit organization managers would prefer to avoid," which include staff time and effort to secure new grants or contracts if revenues are lower than expected (which may not even materialize) and expense reduction to adjust to revenue shocks (Kingma, 1993, p. 109). Importantly, Kingma's (1993) notion of predictability borrows from modern portfolio theory; just as an investor defines risk as the standard deviation (or dispersion) of return from the expected return on a portfolio and chooses a combination of risk and expected return, a nonprofit manager must also select a combination of expected revenues and risks that the organization must bear. "Any increase in expected revenues, whether from an increase in the time and effort devoted to fundraising, grant applications, or requesting additional government revenues, is subject to an increase in risk" (Kingma, 1993, p. 109). Just as risk in a financial portfolio can be measured as the variance and covariance of the assets in the portfolio, risk for nonprofit revenue portfolios can similarly be measured as the variance and covariance of the individual revenue streams. He then tests the theory on a sample of nonprofit child welfare agencies in New York State and finds those more dependent on public funding (which is the dominant funding stream for most of these organizations) have more predictable revenues than those organizations with more revenue streams. Overall, the important contribution of Kingma's (1993) approach is to take risk and return definitions and approaches from finance and apply them to revenue correlations and revenue portfolio risk so that managers could construct revenue portfolios that were predictable.

Jegers (1997) extends Kingma's (1993) analysis to include managerial utility. Specifically, Jegers (1997) notes that the expected revenues from government sources and donations are equally certain in Kingma's (1993) theory.

---

13   Capital funding is discussed in a later section on capital structure (see p. 60).

He states that "if all sources of revenue have equal return, the manager could not increase the rate of return by selecting a riskier revenue source. Therefore, managerial risk aversion ... is irrelevant" (Jegers, 1997, p. 68). He further notes that while investors choose a portfolio with an expected rate of return, for non-profits the entire portfolio is potentially randomly determined; in other words, while the expected rate of return is random for an investor (because he or she owns the assets generating the return, and this is not random), the entire portfolio is for a nonprofit. Further, nonprofit managers may face constraints in building their revenue portfolios that investors would not face. Nevertheless, Jegers (1997) points out that these concerns do not invalidate Kingma (1993), but rather should be factored into future research.

Chang and Tuckman (1991) argue that nonprofits ought to have diversified revenues to minimize the probability of service cutbacks resulting from a revenue shock. The assumption of Chang and Tuckman (1991) is that a shock is most likely to affect just one revenue stream rather than multiple ones; therefore, nonprofits should have several revenue streams to ensure predictability. Chang and Tuckman (1991) essentially examine the special case of Kingma (1993) when all the covariances are zero and the error terms are independent (thus, only one revenue stream is likely affected by a shock). Kingma (1993) is a generalization that recognizes that the standard deviation of a portfolio of revenue streams depends upon the covariances as well the variances. Revenue diversification as a means of reducing financial risk and improving financial health or reducing income volatility was subsequently incorporated into the work of Carroll and Stater (2009), Greenlee and Trussel (2000), Hager (2001), Trussel and Greenlee (2004), and Wicker and Breuer (2014), among others. Mayer and colleagues (2014) incorporate conditional variances into their estimations to show that the type of revenue diversification matters for reducing risk, and that nonprofits are not served well simply by replacing certain revenues with different ones, which would be consistent with the theory presented by Kingma (1993). For example, they find adding investment income to a portfolio increases diversification, but reduces expected revenues while increasing risk, while replacing earned income with donations reduces volatility as well as expected revenues. The results reported by Mayer and colleagues (2014) reinforce the point that increasing revenue diversity by itself does not reduce risk per se.

The notion that revenue diversification alone could improve the financial fortunes of nonprofits was viewed with skepticism by some. Grønbjerg (1992) finds that stable and reliable revenues from only a few funders is associated with high-performing nonprofits. Similarly, Frumkin and Keating (2011) identify several benefits to revenue concentration, including reduced fundraising and administrative costs in earning revenues and revenue growth that exceeds more diversified revenue portfolios. Foster and Fine (2007) argue that revenue concentration supports growth in total revenue (termed "financial capacity") more than revenue diversity does. Chikoto and Neely (2014) similarly find that concentrated revenues lead to growth in total revenues. However, they also find, like Frumkin and Keating (2011), that this growth actually is negatively affected if revenues are too concentrated.

Beyond factors such as risk and return, other research has offered alternative explanations for the benefits of revenue diversification. Bielefeld (1992) and Galaskiewicz and Bielefeld (1998), for example, suggest that nonprofits diversify their funding sources so that they establish more relationships within their communities. These efforts in turn increase community buy-in and increase organizational legitimacy for nonprofits that pursue these strategies.

Current research has begun to explore if the seemingly contradictory findings might reflect differences in how revenue diversification is accomplished rather than just simply diversifying a revenue portfolio. For example, Mayer and colleagues (2014) find that revenue diversity and income volatility changes depend upon the type of diversification pursued by nonprofit agencies. Moving from program service income to donations, for example, negatively affects revenue volatility, while moving from donations to investment income reduces revenue volatility. A meta-analysis by Hung and Hager (2019) finds that revenue diversification does have a small positive effect on organizational financial health (measured as financial capacity—or total assets); how different revenue sources are measured and the methodologies employed in studies influence results significantly. Chikoto and Neely (2014) note that the Herfindahl-Hirschman Index (HHI), a commonly used measure of revenue diversification in the literature, is sensitive to measurement issues. Qu (2016) shows that this index does not even capture correlational diversification measures, which is the whole point of revenue diversification in the first place. Therefore, this line of research might first need to employ common measures that properly operationalize theoretical concepts and data sources to verify what we do and do not know for certain about revenue diversification and nonprofit financial health.

Another consideration is whether portfolio theory applied in the nonprofit domain is comparable to corporations' revenues or projects in the for-profit sector. Modern portfolio theory is based on the idea that an investor may choose investments (the portfolio) that maximize his or her expected return based on a level of market risk (Markowitz, 1952). The investor can construct the portfolio of assets that provide the highest expected returns given some level of acceptable risk; further, the investor can make changes to this portfolio through buying and selling assets to accomplish this optimization. Nonprofits may have little choice about which revenues they earn (as argued from the benefits theory or simply because they might be a membership organization that is dependent upon dues as an example), and may be unable to alter them. Further, while a portfolio reflects a collection of assets which is expected to generate a certain amount of revenue, nonprofit revenues are sometimes derived not from assets but from spending. For example, philanthropy is sought not by investing in particular assets but by spending money on fundraising. If a nonprofit chooses to divest itself of philanthropic revenues, there may be few if any assets to liquidate and reinvest elsewhere.

Ultimately, revenue sources reflect choices made by nonprofit organizations based upon concerns about constituents, stakeholders, and internal issues. Kearns (2007), for instance, notes that such concerns include whether a particular income source is appropriate for an organization (for example, donations from particular funders or fee-for-service charges from particular clients), whether the revenue source can generate sufficient needed resources, the risk of the revenue, the opportunity costs of pursuing the revenue source, and the effect of individual revenue sources on other income sources. Kearns (2007) argues that revenue portfolios are constructed not by organizations, but by people within organizations. These individuals make decisions about revenue streams with their own interpretation about "organizational missions, strategies, goals, constraints, and contingencies" (Kearns, 2007, p. 301).

6.4   *Revenue Portfolios of Membership Organizations*
The revenue portfolios of membership organizations are themselves unique. While these organizations receive donations like other nonprofit agencies, they also charge membership dues and earn income through sales. As noted by Steinberg (2007), the distinctions between these revenue sources for membership organizations are not always clear. Dues in some cases are more like donations because the organization provides nonexcludable collective goods and governance is not a member function (for example, a public radio membership). Other times, dues do confer private benefits to members, who also serve a governance function (such as in many professional associations). However, in both cases, the membership organization reports "dues" as the revenue source. Clearly, this makes distinguishing the pure dues from the donative dues difficult in large databases like those derived from the Form 990.

For 501(c)3 public charities, dues represent an immaterial amount of total revenues—Steinberg (2007) notes that dues are less than 1 percent of total revenues for these nonprofits. This ratio, however, increases for other 501(c) organizations. The size of this ratio also depends upon whether donations are included as "dues" as well. Bowman (2017) finds similar disparities between charitable membership associations and other associations using a differ-ent data source from Steinberg (2007) entirely. Why this difference between types of membership association persists remains an open empirical question. Steinberg (2007) further notes that the price elasticity of membership remains an under-researched area; that is, to what extent associations may alter their dues structure without losing members. Ki and Oh (2018) find that length of association membership, being female, and individuals with more prosocial attitudes tend to donate more to membership associations; interestingly, mem-bership satisfaction had no effect on giving to these nonprofits organizations.

Regardless, dues represent an important revenue source for some nonprofit agencies and voluntary associations. Olson (1965) presumes that joining such associations voluntarily involves an individual balancing the costs of joining (dues) with the benefits; Tschirhart (2006) reviews this literature, including the scholarship with counterarguments. Free-riding remains a concern if the membership association provides nonexcludable benefits. Bowman (2017) finds that every voluntary association reports requiring annual dues from members, although this revenue's importance relative to total revenues varies depending on the mission of the membership association. Charitable asso-ciations rely less on dues (and more on donations) than other membership associations, and larger membership associations actually have more concen-trated revenue portfolios (Bowman, 2017).

6.5   *Revenue Interactions*

6.5.1   Public vs. Private Funds

Related to revenue diversity, another significant line of research in nonprofit sector finance focuses on whether, and the degree to which, different revenue sources affect each other. As the nonprofit sector has transitioned from a largely voluntary contribution revenue base to a more government-financed one, a body of theory developed to predict whether this government revenue would "crowd-in" (that is, attract more) private voluntary donations or "crowd-out" (that is, attract fewer) private voluntary donations. Tinkelman and Neely (2018) identify fifty-four different research studies focusing on the interaction of private voluntary donations and government funding, making it perhaps the most significant area of research in the realm of nonprofit finance.

Further, Tinkelman and Neely (2018, p. 40) provide a summary of the under-lying theoretical assumptions about how government funding might affect voluntary contributions from donors. The general theory is that public goods are produced at the level desired by the median voter and financed through income taxation. If taxes are increased, voters have less after-tax disposable income, and contributions to charities come from this now-reduced pool of income. If such charitable giving is a normal good, then this reduction in income should correspond to less charitable giving (that is, a negative income effect). Further, because there now exists more public goods, there is also a negative substitution effect from the diminishing marginal utility from additional public goods financed through voluntary contributions. However, Steinberg (1987) notes the actual response by contributors is ambiguous because donations may be normal or inferior goods, complements to or substitutes for government spending, and whether provision by others is already above or below the donor's ideal. While many find a small, statistically significant negative crowd-out as predicted, some find positive crowd-in and still others find no results (that is, neither crowd-in nor crowd-out of donations resulting from government financing). The implications of this area of research extend beyond nonprofit finance; Steinberg (1991) notes that significant government crowd-out of private donations implies inefficiency in the funding of public services, whereas crowd-in suggests productivity in government spending. In other words, the crowd-in/crowd-out debate has implications for the system of federalism in the US.

As noted, multiple inquiries exist that test this basic theory. Studies have tested these theories with administrative data (such as the Form 990 data or data on grantees from the National Endowment for the Arts), as well as experimental research designs (for example, de Wit and Bekkers, 2016; Gronberg et al., 2012; Kim and Van Ryzin, 2014, among others). As noted by Vesterlund (2006), experimental studies have a tendency to report larger crowd-out effects, although the results tend to depend on the context and subjects of the experiments. Lu (2016) conducts a meta-analysis on studies in this vein, and ultimately finds no statistically significant correlation between government funding and private donations. By contrast, de Wit and Bekkers (2016) in their own meta-analysis do find a significant negative relationship between government funding and private donations.

The varying results of this body of literature suggest that the act of giving itself is a complex phenomenon, with different motivations and effects for different actors. After examining the literature on charitable giving, Bekkers and Wiepking (2011, p. 936) highlight that "[f]rom the behavior of donors we can infer that they do not care so much about the public benefits generated by their contributions." Rather, these authors find prosocial behavior is rooted in emotions, alleviating guilt, or some other sense of moral obligation. Relatedly, Crumpler and Grossman (2008) even find that individuals will donate to charitable nonprofits even if they determine that their donation will have no effect on organizational outcomes. Therefore, the extant literature suggests that donating may be rooted not in the rational expectation that private actors might supply some desired public good less expensively than government or to meet some unmet desired level of public services, but that such behavior is rooted in basic psychological, sociological, or ethical systems that are difficult to measure and are highly dependent upon the actors involved, even in controlled experiments.

Further, it is not clear that donors use financial information when making decisions to give. Informed giving is uncommon (Krasteva & Yildirim, 2013, 2016) and purchasers seem averse to paying for information that would permit more informed decisions (Null, 2011). Horne, Johnson, and Van Slyke (2005) find that donors are generally unaware of the actual funding sources of nonprofit agencies, although de Wit and Bekkers (2016) do find significant crowd-out of donations when complete financial information is provided in experimental settings. Li and McDougle (2017) survey donors and find that those who use information from rating agencies are influenced in their decision to volunteer, but this has no correlation with donating money to nonprofits; however, they do not test whether public funds affect giving or volunteering in their analysis. Moreover, if most donations are made by large donors (as documented in Clotfelter, 2002), this lack of information found in the literature is perhaps less salient. A significant donor can now easily, and at low cost, inform him or herself about the finances of a potential grantee.

Beyond financial information, the lack of information on programmatic quality may influence donor giving. The literature has long recognized this information problem, and some have suggested that government funding might serve as a signal for program quality (see, for example, Hughes & Luksetich, 1999; Payne, 2001; Rose-Ackerman, 1986). Crowd-in, therefore, might best be understood as a nonprofit receiving a general "stamp of approval" from a government funder, which serves as a proxy for acceptable program quality and management. As a result, donors contribute more.

Still others have suggested that economies of scale have an influence on the crowd-in/crowd-out debate. Rose-Ackerman (1986) suggests that government funding might improve the marginal productivity of donations, and crowd-in additional contributions because of this improved efficiency. Lee (2006) notes that private donations have only one layer of administrative costs (at the nonprofit organizational level) while government funding has two (at the nonprofit organizational and government levels); this assumes the donation derives from an individual rather than a private institution, however. Relaxing this assumption would change this calculus. Other studies have found a curvilinear relationship between government funding and donations (for example, Borgonovi, 2006; Brooks, 2000; Nikolova, 2015). These authors find crowd-in at low levels of government funding and crowd-out at higher levels. These findings may support the notion that government funding serves as a quality signal at low levels of funding, but donors view high levels of government funding as transforming the nonprofit agency essentially into a tax-supported public organization—resulting in less voluntary giving to the nonprofit. Andreoni and Payne (2011a) also point out that much of the literature examining crowd-in or crowd-out of donations ought to focus instead on net donations (that is, contributions less fundraising expenses). They find accounting for reduced fundraising expenses explains a significant amount of reported crowd-out.

Relatedly, Andreoni (1998) posits that "leadership givers"—that is, funders that launch fundraising efforts, especially capital campaigns—can spur giving to nonprofit charities because of increasing returns at low levels of service provisions. Such leadership giving also might serve as a signal that the nonprofit agency is high-quality, and very large gifts from the wealthy may be needed to ensure this signal is credible (Andreoni, 2006). Another issue with donations is that they may be conditional upon other donations—that is, matching grants. Karlan and List (2007) find that the price of giving changes as match rates change, although Meier and Frey (2004) find that lower match values do not induce more giving. Similar results are found in Rondeau and List (2008), while Landry et al. (2010) further find that such matching can signal quality and keep first-time donors engaged.

Beyond theoretical issues, the literature has also addressed empirical concerns. Seaman (2006), for example, models donor and government funding as simultaneous equations rather than assuming exogeneity. Lu (2016) finds that reported results vary in part due to endogeneity corrections, or the lack thereof. Others have tried to overcome the potential endogeneity of government funding using instrumental variables (Andreoni & Payne, 2011a, 2011b; Gruber & Hungerman, 2007; Hungerman, 2005), or lagged variables (Horne, 2005). Still others have used shocks to examine the crowd-in/crowd-out relationship. For example, Dokko (2009) uses Congressional party changes—and the subsequent change in arts funding through the National Endowment for the Arts—to examine the effect on contributions.

Data limitations also exist. The Form 990, the most common source of financial data on the sector, is limited to larger nonprofit agencies and does not even cover informal associations. Further, the Form 990 data do not comport with GAAP (Fischer, Gordon, & Kraut, 2002). Therefore, what is included as government funding and private contributions are not consistently reported across the sector. For example, some organizations may report pledges are revenues in the year pledged, while others may report the revenues only upon receipt of the pledge. Further, the Form 990 does not distinguish between private donations that are unrestricted and those that have donor restrictions attached to them.[14] The current literature assumes that the donor decision is to donate to a non-profit agency or to withhold donating to the agency. However, the donor has another choice which cannot be explored with Form 990 data—to donate and restrict the contribution to time or purpose. Hence, if the donor is concerned that a nonprofit agency is becoming "too public" and will not spend his or her donation as desired, the donor can restrict the use of the donation and remove managerial discretion. But this choice is completely unexplored in the current literature because of the lack of visibility on restricted donations.

Further, government funding is not only in the form of grants, which would be reported on the Form 990 on line 1e. Earned income derived from governments are not included on this line item, and these income sources are vitally important to many nonprofit agencies. For example, Medicare and Medicaid are earned-income sources that make up significant portions of many health care organizations' total revenues; many social service agencies have contracts to provide particular services (such as foster care) for governments. Do donors care about these revenue sources in determining where their contributions go, or do they only care about government grants? The Form 990 provides inadequate insight into these other publicly supported revenue streams because they are largely lumped together with "program service revenue" (line 2 of the Form 990). Some may even report these earned revenues as government grants, while others report them as program service revenue making the data issue even more concerning. Zhao and Lu (2019) open an interesting line of inquiry by asking whether different types of government grants might crowd-in or crowd-out other government grants. They find evidence that concentrated government funding from a large funder crowds out smaller government funding. This approach to within-revenue source revenue diversification and interaction may uncover currently unknown effects, but data must be sufficiently granular to permit such an analysis. The overall issue, nevertheless, remains that data limitations exist that limit the questions that can be asked, the development of theory, and may influence the results already published.

6.5.2 Donations vs. Commercial Revenues

The other significant body of literature about revenue interactions focuses on how donation revenues change as a nonprofit earns more commercial revenues.

---

14 Basically, the Form 990 reports the stock value of unrestricted, temporarily restricted, and permanently restricted net assets on the balance sheet. It does not report the flow variables that measure the rate at which restricted donations are recorded. The changes from the balance sheet accounts only reflect the net effect of additions and subtractions.

In other words, as an organization moves from donative to commercial—to use Hansmann's (1980) framework—this literature examines whether or not donations are crowded out or not.

James (1983) models nonprofits as pursuing some activities that were inherently not profitable, requiring cross-subsidization from more profitable activities. Schiff and Weisbrod (1991) expand upon this model and posit that managers prefer the subsidized output and dislike the commercial good. Tuckman and Chang (2006), as but one example, point out that some nonprofit museums receive far more operating revenue from gift shops than they do from admission or donation revenues. Gift shop revenues, in this example, permit museums to keep admission costs lower than they would otherwise need to be, to keep longer operating hours than they could in the absence of the gift shop revenue, and to potentially offer more programs than they could without commercial revenue. Beyond the gift shop example, universities have established partnerships with for-profit companies (see, for example, Powell & Owen-Smith, 1998), hospitals have engaged with private pharmaceutical companies (Tuckman and Chang, 2006) and established their own for-profit subsidiaries to generate additional revenue or even converted to for-profits (Sloan, 1998), museums (in addition to gift shops) now also sometimes operate restaurants and parking garages (Strom, 2002), the American Association of Retired Persons (a membership nonprofit organization) receives royalties from insurance products sold to members (Young, 1998), etc. These examples assume that commercial activity supports the provision of nonprofit outputs. Eckel and Steinberg (1993), however, did posit that these activities could be used for managerial benefits as well as public good provision.

Perhaps unsurprisingly, Weisbrod (1998) and Cordes and Weisbrod (1998) point to the increase in nonprofit commercial revenues since the late 1980s, caused perhaps by cutbacks in federal funding to nonprofits in the 1980s. For example, Salamon (1997) estimates that cuts to public welfare programs during the late 1970s through the 1980s reduced nonprofit revenues by $38 billion in total. During a similar time period, Hodgkinson and Weitzman (2001) report that private contributions dropped—from 26 percent of revenues in 1977 to 18 percent in 1992. As a result, some speculate nonprofits turned towards commercial activity to make up for the loss in public and private funding (see Eikenberry & Kluver, 2004, for example). Others, notably Foster and Bradach (2005), counter that commercial activity may have increased initially due to reductions in other revenues, but commercial revenue in nonprofits was essentially flat as a share of revenues during the 1990s (although they did not examine whether this was because other revenues might have increased as well). Kerlin and Pollak (2011) examine the 1982 to 2002 time period and find evidence that commercial activity in nonprofits did generate more revenues, but find no evidence that this change was caused by declines in other revenue sources from governments or private donors.

In addition to the notion that commercial activity might be a reaction to other revenues declining, there is the concern that commercial activity may crowd-out voluntary contributions. Theoretically, donors might view commercial nonprofits as less deserving of contributions than those nonprofits in need. Perhaps these donors feel that commercial nonprofits are financially healthy enough that their contributions might be more impactful elsewhere, or perhaps they view the commercial activity as organizational mission drift. From the organization's perspective, earning commercial revenues may permit it to fundraise less. Regardless, the commercial activity might have a negative effect on private giving. On the flip side, other donors might view the commercial activity positively and donate more—causing a crowd-in effect. Perhaps these donors wish to reward organizational risk-taking or entrepreneurialism, perhaps they view the commercial activity as better securing the financial future of the nonprofits, or perhaps the sales activity is complementary to donations. From the organization's perspective, commercial revenue might be spent on extra fundraising that draws in additional private giving. Overall, then, commercial activity—just like government funding described before—might have either crowd-in or crowd-out effects on voluntary contributions.

Scholarship has examined this relationship seeking to understand the effects of commercialism on private giving to nonprofits. Kingma (1995) analyzes the commercial activities of the American Red Cross—charges from health and safety services net of health and safety product costs spent on these services. He finds that earnings from these services have large negative effects on private donations, suggesting significant crowd-out of private giving from commercial activity. Kingma (1995) also finds, however, that donation increases serve to reduce profits from commercial activity, which is similar to findings in Jacobs and Wilder (1984). Such a finding may also lend insights to theories about nonprofit cross-subsidization of services, since such donations in these cases seem to subsidize the health and safety services of the organization. Segal and Weisbrod (1997) note that the estimated interaction between commercial and donative revenues depend on the statistical estimation technique employed. Employing fixed effects, they show a negative relationship (crowd-out) between commercial and donative revenues, but mixed results when these are not included. Hughes and Luksetich (1999) analyze the interrelationships of museums' revenues and employ a two-stage least squares system of equations to address simultaneity concerns. Unlike some other analyses, they find a positive and significant relationship (crowd-in) between private support and earned income. Okten and Weisbrod (2000) estimate the elasticity of donations to a number of factors, including revenues from other sources. They find no statistical effect (neither crowd-in nor crowd-out) between the two revenue sources; in two subsectors (higher education and scientific research) they find marginal evidence of crowd-in, but the effect is weak. Yetman and Yetman (2003) examine whether taxable activities operated by nonprofits crowd-out donations or not. They find significant crowd-out effects for arts, culture, humanities, human service, and public benefit organizations, but not for education or medical nonprofits. The results further suggest that the loss of donations is outweighed by the financial benefits of the taxable activities. The authors also find no effect between donations and tax-exempt commercial activity. These results suggest different effects for different sectors as well as donor differentiation between related and unrelated taxable activities in many cases. Beyond the US, Wong, Chua, and Vasoo (1998) analyze revenue interactions in a sample of nonprofit organizations in Singapore. Among their findings, revenue derived from commercial and investment activity crowds out private donations in general. However, these same revenues crowd-in private donations when the sample is limited to those organizations that are members of the Community Chest of Singapore (CCS), which raises money and distributes these funds to member agencies. Perhaps donors find that the CCS provides a level of oversight to ensure donations are used for charitable purposes despite commercial activity, or perhaps donors simply have more trust that the CCS will distribute donations to the "best" agencies.

This line of research will benefit from future efforts to test existing theory. Data that separate commercial activity more finely (as in Yetman & Yetman, 2003) are likely to reveal more nuanced approaches to giving by donors. In addition, data that permit researchers to analyze nonprofits at a consolidated level—as in audited financial reports rather than at legal entity level as in the Form 990—might uncover interesting results; because commercial activities might be established as separate legal entities by nonprofits, current analyses that rely upon Form 990 data are forced to treat these as separate independent organizations rather than one related entity. If research could examine the consolidated operations of these nonprofits with donative and commercial revenues, we might gain additional insight into the cross-subsidization of programs by nonprofits. Further, as noted earlier, existing research assumes donors can only give or not give; data that include information on donor restrictions might reveal that some donors change the type of contribution they give to increasingly commercial nonprofits by limiting it to spending on charitable outputs.

6.5.3   Recent Innovations in Nonprofit Finance

The nonprofit sector continues to develop and innovate. In the past, donative organizations oftentimes sought earned-income strategies to increase potential revenues; James (1983), relatedly, pointed out that nonprofits cross-subsidize certain outputs by generating surpluses on other outputs. Recent financing innovations may not yet have significant research devoted to them or explore potential first- or second-order effects to nonprofit financial health or mission, but still warrant mention. Most basically, recent inventions in different legal forms have emerged. While nonprofits are primarily mission-driven (Steinberg & Galle, 2018), recent entrepreneurs and social innovators have occasionally found the existing legal infrastructure of the sector limiting in their ability to effect their desired changes. As a result, innovative legal forms have emerged to address social concerns traditionally in the purview of the nonprofit sector, forms that exist somewhere between the nonprofit and for-profit spaces. While nonprofits have long generated extra income from business activities (such as thrift stores or gaming activities that generate profits to support mission services), different social enterprise forms have emerged to attempt to overcome failures in the commercial and charitable sectors.

The term "social enterprises" is itself confusing, and how these differ from traditional business, nonprofit, and even governmental forms is oftentimes elusive. Young and Longhofer (2016) include six organizational forms in their conception of social enterprises:

1. Social businesses, defined as a company devoted to addressing a social problem and earning profits that are reinvested in providing more services rather than distributed as dividends to investors.
2. Social cooperatives, defined as a voluntary autonomous group formed to meet some common need, which in this case explicitly includes broader social objectives.
3. Social innovations, defined as novel solutions to social problems that are in some way superior to current solutions. These innovations might be organizational, or they might be new programs by existing organizations or simply new policies or practices by existing organizations.
4. Socially responsible corporations, which adhere to values consistent with a broad swathe of society, not just investors.
5. Benefit corporations, defined as entities that benefit society and the environment and have higher standards of accountability and transparency compared to other corporations.
6. Sustainable businesses, which seek profitability while protecting or enhancing social welfare.

Reiser and Dean (2013) note that social enterprises can be found in both nonprofit and for-profit forms. The nonprofit form may protect mission well, but lacks access to adequate capital frequently. In contrast, the for-profit social enterprise has better access to capital, but may end up sacrificing social aims. Steinberg (2015) notes that for-profit firms do provide social goods (which might enhance or detract from profits). These organizations are considered more vulnerable to contract failure or loss of trustworthiness compared to nonprofits (Steinberg, 2006). This tension between organizational form has led to increasingly diverse structures to address seemingly intractable societal needs.

As a result, hybrid forms have developed such as the low-profit limited liability company (L3C) and the flexible-purpose corporation (FPC) (Young & Lecy, 2014), although these hybrid forms may not in themselves solve the friction between profits and mission. Rather than legal form addressing this natural tension between money and mission, Reiser and Dean (2013) describe a financing vehicle that seeks to do both—Flexible Low Yield (FLY) paper. FLY paper is a debt instrument in which the entrepreneur retains ownership control (and its accompanying social mission) and the investors accept a return that takes into account not just financial risk, but social returns as well (the "double bottom line"). However, if the entrepreneur tries to maximize personal reward by selling his or her stock, FLY paper investors basically have the right to have their debt converted to equity at very favorable rates of return. Hence, the focus is not on new entities or structures, but on new financing arrangements—which may be more sustainable across sectors. FLY paper provides investors with both a financial and social return, and attempts to ameliorate some of the agency problems that might exist in these ventures.

Other innovations in nonprofit funding includes social impact bonds (SIBS). In these arrangements, which have occurred most frequently in the US and United Kingdom, but also elsewhere, private or philanthropic investors provide funding to nonprofit service providers, usually in the form of start-up funds (Fischer & Richter, 2017). Outcome funders, which are usually public agencies, pay these investors a contracted amount if some agreed-upon outcome is achieved (Pandey et al., 2018). These outcomes might be reduced recidivism for prisoners, increased labor market participation for job training programs, and so on. But importantly, the outcomes are measured through cash savings to the public agency. Thus, new interventions that reduce the costs of the public program (especially with high-risk or high-utilization populations) will result in returns, but those that do not will not cost the government additional money. Despite their name, SIBS are more similar to government grants than debt instruments (which are discussed in detail later), because there is no obligation by the service provider (the nonprofit typically) to repay the amount used to finance the program. Faulk and colleagues (2019) further find that the use of SIBS by nonprofits does not crowd-out philanthropic support. Interestingly, they also find donor resistance to for-profit substitutes for nonprofit service provision. This might be because ultimately, donors trust nonprofits to provide better-quality services or to not distribute profits or be driven by altruism rather than purely monetary concerns. Hence, ironically, the move towards unique organizational forms to solve persistent problems may end up circling back to the original nonprofit charitable form because of the nondistribution constraint. Finally, SIBS' primary value might be that they are well suited for particular types of investors who may not have otherwise put their money into direct service provision. If SIBS draw in these marginal impact investors while not pushing out existing donors or lenders, they are likely to maintain a role for addressing particular but limited social needs.

Another area of nonprofit finance in need of additional research is donor-advised funds (DAFs). These funds essentially act like a personal checking account, in which a donor irrevocably gives money to some intermediary (a sponsor) who manages the assets; the donor receives an immediate tax deduction for the gift and advises the intermediary to which public charities money should be directed (Heist & Vance-McMullen, 2019). These funds have grown significantly in recent years, reaching over $100 billion in assets. As DAFs have grown, controversy has emerged. For example, critics note the lack of transparency around grant recipients—whereas foundations must disclose recipients, no such requirement exists for DAFs. Further, money accumulated in DAFs face no regulation that they ever be distributed, unlike foundations that face minimum spending rules (Cantor, 2018). DAFs have been criticized as tools of wealthy donors to receive tax breaks with minimal social benefits given in return that slow the flow of funds to nonprofits. And, when money does arrive, the nonprofit oftentimes is unsure who the donor actually is (Olen, 2017). Data limitations preclude many significant analyses beyond simple descriptive statistics. Nevertheless, understanding if and how these DAFs alter the existing findings on donor behavior and revenue interactions (crowd-in/crowd-out) seem like natural and important extensions of our current knowledge base.

7   Uses of Funds

This section describes where nonprofits spend money in the production of goods and services, and then focuses on the difficulty of measuring the outputs and outcomes produced by nonprofits. Here, it is argued that this complexity leads to the use of proxy measures of efficiency that incentivize certain behaviors, such as cost shifting and misreporting.

7.1   *Overview*

Nonprofits use the funds they acquire in the production of goods and services, just like all other organizations. In other words, nonprofits produce total outputs from their chosen inputs, and these outputs are as varied as the sector is. Based on 2017 data, nearly one-third of nonprofit agencies that file the Form 990 report no personnel expenses in the forms of wages, payroll taxes, or fringe benefits.[15] But for those that do report personnel expenses, the median nonprofit agency spent nearly 43 percent of their total expenses on staff. Variation exists between the major nonprofit subsectors, as evidenced in Table 2. Perhaps unsurprisingly, education and health—two subsectors with perhaps more licensing and occupational training requirements than other subsectors—have the highest level of compensation as a percentage of total expenses. In all cases, larger nonprofit agencies report higher percentages of compensation relative to total spending.

TABLE 2   Personnel expenses as percentage of spending, 2017

	Compensation as percentage of expenses (median)	Compensation as percentage of expenses if reporting paid staff
All	27.1%	43.0%
Subsector (NTMAJ5)		
Arts, culture, and humanities	29.2%	40.0%
Education	30.2%	54.6%
Health	41.7%	52.8%
Human services	29.9%	46.4%
Other	19.0%	37.7%

SOURCE: AUTHOR'S CALCULATIONS. DERIVED FROM IRS EXEMPT ORGANIZATIONS BUSINESS MASTER FILE EXTRACT (EO BMF) FY 2015–2017

---

15   Defined here as compensation of current officers, compensation of other employees, other salaries and wages, pension plan contributions, other employee benefits, and payroll taxes.

TABLE 3   Estimates of capital usage by nonprofit agencies, 2017

	Occupancy expenses as percentage of expenses (median)	Fixed assets as percentage of total assets (median)
All	8.5%	21.1%
Subsector (NTMAJ5)		
Arts, culture, and humanities	10.8%	18.2%
Education	9.1%	16.5%
Health	6.7%	16.5%
Human services	9.9%	36.9%
Other	7.3%	9.5%

SOURCE: AUTHOR'S CALCULATIONS. DERIVED FROM IRS EXEMPT ORGANIZATIONS BUSINESS MASTER FILE EXTRACT (EO BMF) FY 2015–2017

Estimating capital acquisition and usage is difficult from the Form 990 because no cash flow statement is required. Also, some nonprofit agencies purchase capital outright, some finance it through borrowing, and some rent large assets instead of purchasing them. Here, two proxies are employed to estimate capital usage. The first measures the costs of occupancy—specifically, rent expenses, depreciation, and interest costs—as a percentage of total expenses. This measure gets closest to an estimate of the usage of capital in the production of services. The second measures the amount of property, plant, and equipment relative to total assets. While not a measure of usage, it shows how intensive fixed assets are in the sector. Neither is perfect, but better data are unavailable from the Form 990.

Estimates of both measures are included in Table 3. The estimates suggest low reported utilization of occupancy costs or fixed asset intensity. When the data are examined more closely, both reveal that larger nonprofit agencies have increasing measures relative to smaller nonprofit agencies. This might suggest that smaller nonprofits either do not have physical locations, work out of space acquired in the past (and therefore fully depreciated), donated space (because the Form 990 does not include space-in-kind data unlike audited financial statements), or incorrect reporting of these expense and asset amounts.[16] Nevertheless, the data show that compensation and occupancy

16   Also, financial statements only report accounting costs and do not include opportunity costs, which are relevant here as well.

costs, when taken together, represent significant portions of nonprofit agency spending. The remaining expenses would include professional service fees (for consultants and auditors, for example), travel expenses, advertising expenses, insurance expenses, miscellaneous expenses, and so on. Spending is presumed to be consistent with generating outcomes consistent with the nonprofit organization's mission.

7.2   *The Problem of Measuring Outcomes*

What is most interesting about nonprofit production is not the specifics about these inputs, however. Rather, much existing theory notes that nonprofit agencies are important in a mixed economy because they produce unobserved outcomes. Arrow (1963) claims nonprofits are more trustworthy because the concept of earning a profit could discourage the provision of high-quality health care services—a sector with a significant nonprofit presence. Given the difficulty of observing or judging these services, nonprofit status helps mitigate client/patient quality concerns. Continuing on this theme, Hansmann (1980) theorizes that nonprofits have a competitive advantage over for-profits in the production of these unobservable outcomes because of the nondistribution constraint. Because nonprofits could not distribute profits to owners, donors and other third-party financiers (that is, those not directly receiving services from the nonprofit) would have more trust that the nonprofit would not reduce quality or quantity of outputs in order to profit. In other words, the nondistribution constraint contributes to a reduction in producer opportunism where evaluation of quantity or quality of services provided to clients but financed by other third parties (such as donors) is difficult or impossible. Hansmann (1996) notes that the nonprofit form serves "as a crude but effective consumer protection device in severe situations of asymmetric information." Nonprofits in this understanding overcome "contract failure" in which for-profits have incentives to take advantage of consumers due to asymmetric information. Nonprofits, then, exist to "foster trustworthiness" because the nondistribution constraint reduces this incentive (Steinberg & Gray, 1993).

Contract failure on its own, however, does not explain the emergence of the nonprofit sector. Steinberg and Gray (1993) note that government also faces a nondistribution constraint and might also suitably reduce contract failure incentives. They note Weisbrod's (1975) theory that governments provide public goods according to the desire of the median voter and that nonprofits exist to supplement or direct resources to organizations for other citizens (those above the median voter or those with difference preferences), among other reasons government provision might not as effectively reduce incentives for contact failure. Further, Hansmann (1980) and Young (1981) argue that entrepreneurs

self-sort into industry sectors, and those more agreeable to the nondistribution constraint will form nonprofits. James (1986) expands this self-selection
mechanism to religious and ideological nonprofits, but the result is the same.
Her theory helps explain the presence of nonprofits as a response to contract
failure. Finally, contract failure theory on its own does not explain the existence of mixed economies with nonprofit and for-profit firms. However, even
with the presence of "for-profits in disguise" (as might be the case in nonprofit
health care), Hirth (1999) finds that the nondistribution constraint is sufficient
to not only provide quality services in nonprofit organizations, but also has a
spillover effect on for-profit participants.

Trustworthiness, it would seem, requires knowledge that a provider is nonprofit, and yet the literature is decidedly mixed on whether consumers are
aware of this distinction and know whether particular organizations are for-
profit or nonprofit. Schlesinger, Mitchell, and Gray (2004) surveyed studies
about nonprofit trustworthiness and found mixed results; importantly about
one-third of survey participants did not understand differences in organizational form. Handy and colleagues (2010) find in a survey of college students
a preference to purchase health care and education from nonprofits; however,
these same students were frequently unable to discern the organizational form
(nonprofit, for-profit, or government) of the provider. Similarly, McDougle
(2014) finds that low-income individuals and clients that are racial minorities
prefer public or nonprofit health care provision, but also were less aware of
nonprofit status.

Nevertheless, the trustworthiness of nonprofits relative to for-profits is a
key feature in much theoretical consideration of the sector (Weisbrod, 1988;
Weisbrod & Schlesinger, 1986). Konrath and Handy (2018) find trust is a key factor that determines to which nonprofit a donor contributes. Similarly, Bekkers
and Bowman (2009) find more trusting individuals and more altruistic individuals are more likely to maintain confidence in nonprofit organizations.
Weisbrod (1988) notes that nonprofit organizations are precisely the type of
organization better suited to produce outcomes that are unobservable or too
costly to observe.

There still remains uncertainty to the extent nonprofits succeed in addressing contract failure. After all, nonprofits are still likely to be providing services
in which quality is difficult to observe. As a result, donors and consumers
search for signals that particular individual nonprofit organizations might be
trustworthy. One avenue by which nonprofits signal they are good and trustworthy stewards of money is through financial reports and ratios. Mitchell
(2017) posits that trust is signaled through fiscal propriety—specifically
through program expense ratios that are high, and also through low reported

overhead spending. However, Anthony, Dearden, and Bedford (1984) and Weisbrod (1988) both warned against relying upon a proxy measure of effectiveness rather than something else.

Despite the warnings, external stakeholders frequently rely upon these measures to assume nonprofits are behaving properly and maintaining trust. Garven, Hofmann, and McSwain (2016) detail that nonprofits are frequently evaluated using the program spending ratio, despite its limited usefulness in evaluating performance. Mitchell and Calabrese (2018) note that no evidence exists that reduced overhead spending results in nonprofits being more impactful or effective, or reduces total costs per outcome (that is, improves efficiency). In fact, these measures of program spending as a percentage of total spending include no output or outcome measures, meaning it lacks validity as a measure of effectiveness or efficiency. Coupet and Berrett (2019) analyze the efficiency of Habitat for Humanity affiliates and find that overhead ratios are negatively correlated with actual efficiency measures, suggesting these constructs are not synonymous.

Nevertheless, the difficulty in measuring outcomes in the nonprofit sector had led to observers ignoring the advice of earlier scholars and relying upon these cost ratios instead. Nonprofit agencies with higher overhead spending are presumed to divert resources from current programmatic spending and direct it instead to wasteful overhead spending (Tinkelman, 2006).

As a result, important stakeholders analyze and report on nonprofit cost ratios, defined in various ways. The administrative expense ratio is defined as the percentage of total spending devoted to the management and general function of the organization. The overhead ratio starts with the administrative expense ratio and includes fundraising costs as well. The ratio of program spending to total expenses is sometimes referred to as the "price" of giving, with overheads treated similarly to a tax. These ratios are all very easy to calculate and data are available from the publicly reported Form 990. None of these ratios examines or measures actual outcomes, however.

Despite these warnings from decades ago, important stakeholders that might influence the flow of donations to nonprofit agencies report on these cost ratios for individual organizations routinely. CharityWatch, a long-established watchdog that exists to provide information to donors, reports on program spending ratios as part of its rating process, asserting that organizations that fail to meet their standards (75 percent spent on programs) are inefficient. The Better Business Bureau's Wise Giving Alliance is slightly more generous by allowing a 65 percent program spending ratio to meet their standards. Charity Navigator similarly limits overhead spending to less than 20 percent to be considered efficient (Mitchell & Calabrese, 2018). *Forbes* magazine ranks large nonprofit agencies annually, and considers overhead spending in excess of 20 percent unreasonable when assigning rankings. In Oregon, state regulators will disqualify any nonprofit with an overhead rate in excess of 70 percent (Mayer, 2016). Rankings and measures of the "best nonprofits" fundamentally ignore outcomes and focus (at least in part) on proxies that are poor measures of efficiency and effectiveness. Nonprofit agencies, then, face the incentive of reporting use of funds in detail, in the form of financial information, that conforms with these expectations in order to attract future revenues.

Because the public is told that low overhead is better than high overhead, perhaps unsurprisingly research consistently shows that nonprofit agencies that report higher overhead rates receive less donations. Such results are reported in Callen (1994), Gordon, Knock, and Nealy (2009), Jacobs and Marudas (2009), Khanna, Posnett, and Sandler (1995), Khanna and Sandler (2000), Marudas (2004, 2015), Tinkelman (1998, 1999), and Tinkelman and Mankaney (2007), among others. One of the few exceptions to this literature is Steinberg (1986b), in which he refutes the notion that overhead ratios are components of the price of giving and shows the price of giving is independent from these cost ratios. Including these in the price of giving confuses average and marginal costs—because the financial reports can only provide data that leads to averages. Hence, donors will not know all relevant parameters, which makes aversion to these overhead costs irrational. Steinberg (1986b) further demonstrates that including cost ratio measures into predictions about donations produces statistically insignificant results. Nevertheless, some funders have similarly imposed limits on the overhead they will cover. As a result, nonprofits face limitations on how they can recoup administrative and fundraising costs (Gneezy, Keenan, & Gneezy, 2014).

Unsurprisingly, organizations respond to incentives. Because of the widespread belief that overhead is wasteful and should not be funded and because these costs are frequently not paid for from funders, nonprofit agencies have reduced real and reported spending on these costs. Lecy and Searing (2015) comment on the nonprofit "starvation cycle" in which overhead is minimized to such an extent that even mission-related activities are negatively affected; in their study, they find evidence of declines in administrative spending even though fundraising spending increases. Overhead might be thought of as support centers for the parts of the nonprofit entity that performs direct services. Reducing this support, then, might lead to actual inefficiencies in the organization. Wing and Hager (2004) and Gregory and Howard (2009) find evidence that low overhead reduces effectiveness, which undermines the mission of the nonprofit agency. Young and Steinberg (1995) find minimizing fundraising costs leads to inefficient fundraising in which nonprofit agencies fail to raise donations until marginal costs equal marginal revenues. In addition to fundraising inefficiency, Steinberg and Morris (2010) find that minimizing fundraising costs can result in increases in other administrative costs (such as compliance and regulatory costs), as well as solicitations that lack adequate transparency. In the German context, Schubert and Boenigk (2019) find that declines in overhead costs is rooted in cuts to fundraising expenses and not to other administrative costs (in contrast to Lecy & Searing's 2015 American context findings). Greenlee and Trussel (2000), Tevel, Katz, and Brock (2015), and Trussel (2002) find weakened financial positions resulting from low overhead.

Because of the incentive to report low overhead, nonprofit agencies have reduced spending in this area. However, nonprofit organizations have also turned to expense manipulation to comport with perceived standards. There exists a robust body of evidence that nonprofit agencies are incentivized to shift overhead costs toward program services to achieve desired program spending ratios. In an experiment, Khumawala, Parsons, and Gordon (2005) find that financial statement users give donations to nonprofit agencies almost entirely based on the cost of fundraising. Although they find no evidence that joint costs (that is, those costs incurred to provide both overhead and direct programmatic service—such as a fundraising effort that also has an education component to it) are used to alter these cost ratios, the authors do raise the concern that savvy nonprofit managers might use these joint costs to alter reported cost ratios and increase marginal donations away from other organizations. Relatedly, Qu and Daniel (2019) report on an experiment in which potential donors do exhibit overhead aversion, but this aversion can actually be mitigated through various forms of framing. For example, if the overhead is described as building capacity, donors seem less concerned; further, removing the word overhead from the appeal increases giving to the nonprofit. Buchheit and Parsons (2006) find experimental evidence that donors are most sensitive to the reported program spending ratio, suggesting that donors have a negative interpretation about overhead. They also find that only a minority of donors request financial information, and data on service efforts and accomplishments are thought by potential donors as decision-useful, even though no evidence finds them significant. In contrast, Newman, Shniderman, Cain, and Sevel (2019) find experimental evidence that donors firmly committed to a nonprofit's cause are less swayed by overhead spending, suggesting that these cost ratios are most important to marginal donors rather than devoted ones.

While the above studies rely upon experiments to uncover donor behavior around cost ratios, others use administrative and financial data to similarly examine the issue. Baber, Daniel, and Roberts (2002) find evidence that changes in program spending that make the nonprofit appear in a more favorable light are associated with increases in managerial compensation, providing an incentive to alter functional expense reporting. Wing and colleagues (2006) find errors in reporting expense classifications of Form 990 and audited financial statements. Krishnan, Yetman, and Yetman (2006) find evidence that nonprofit agencies underreport fundraising expenses, and this is partially explained by managerial incentives to report lower fundraising costs. Jones and Roberts (2006) do find evidence that nonprofits strategically allocate joint costs to influence reported changes in cost ratios. Keating, Parsons, and Roberts (2008) find that nearly three-quarters of nonprofits misreport telemarketing fundraising expenses in financial disclosures, reducing reported administrative expenses. Again, the implication is that nonprofit organizations have an incentive to misreport these expenses to look "more efficient." Krishnan and Yetman (2011) find evidence that nonprofit hospitals in California facing pressures to appear "efficient" accomplish this by shifting costs from administrative and fundraising categories to program categories; the authors compare the results of Form 990 filings with regulatory disclosures required of hospitals within the state. Yetman and Yetman (2012) find that, beginning after 1998, donors began discounting obviously incorrect cost ratios reported by nonprofit organizations. This discount varies by financial information user sophistication and is not universally found. Qu, Steinberg, and Burger (2019), using Benford's Law borrowed from forensic accounting, find that nonprofits with positive fundraising and administrative expenses have lower occurrences of suspicious filings. Relatedly, although not about overhead versus program spending ratios, Eldenburg and Vines (2004) find that nonprofit hospitals engage in expense reclassification, but specifically between bad debt and charity care expenses. In this case, reported spending is deemed more "charitable," making the nonprofit worthier of voluntary contributions.

Unlike for-profit organizations that have a common metric to judge performance—profitability—nonprofits lack any similar meaningful measure of outcomes—the ultimate use of their funds. Because nonprofits must maintain trustworthiness since outcomes are not observable, external evaluators have relied upon cost ratios to measure efficiency and effectiveness. In other words, the lack of outcome measures leads to nonprofits being judged on their inputs. Nonprofits react to this incentive by reducing actual spending on overhead services deemed to be wasteful and noncritical. Nonprofits also might alter financial disclosures so that reported cost ratios appear better than they are in actuality. These improved cost ratios are interpreted as improved efficiency, making the nonprofit organization more trustworthy.

8   Slack, Working Capital, and Reserves

This section describes various components of finance used to ensure the smooth operation of the organization. The various components are described with appropriate literature outlined. The difficulties nonprofits face in accumulating and using these financial tools are also described. In addition, the section addresses foundations, how they differ from other nonprofits, and relevant literature about their financial operations.

8.1   *Overview*
While nonprofits are bound by the nondistribution constraint, organizations have significant discretion about how any excess funds—that is, money left over after paying for organizational costs—are used. Bowman (2011) notes that the term "slack" frequently has negative connotations in the management sciences. However, despite profit maximization not necessarily being the prime goal of all nonprofits, these organizations may find it advantageous to accumulate surpluses (that is, revenues in excess of expenses). Slack becomes useful to take quick advantage of potential growth opportunities, to expand service offerings, or to mitigate the risks of running out of money due to unforeseen circumstances. While slack has benefits, there are also costs. For example, growth opportunities may not be properly vetted as they might be when outside funds are employed, managers may enrich themselves through perquisites, and operations may not be as efficient as possible. Nevertheless, some amount of slack may help nonprofits deal with routine business operations that can be costly and disruptive if an organization lacks sufficient liquidity to handle business cycles.

A key component of generating sufficient slack and liquidity are annual operating profits. Hansmann (1981) points out that one justification to exempt nonprofits from corporate income taxes is to subsidize capital formation in nonprofits. Because nonprofits may be more efficient compared to for-profits in providing services characterized by contract failure, the subsidy provided by tax exemption might be offset by efficiency gains from the growth in nonprofit suppliers. These operating profits serve as an internal source of funds that can also be used for long-term investments. Profits are especially important to nonprofits because unlike for-profit entities that have a robust and well-developed equity market to turn to, nonprofits do not. Further, Hansmann (1981) notes that nonprofits face distinct limits on borrowing as a source of capital; similar to for-profits, nonprofits are unable to borrow all of their capital needs and lenders tend towards more conservative lending with nonprofits given the "awkwardness of the control relationship" (p. 73) when the nonprofit borrower is significantly financed with leverage.

The nonprofit sector has unique accounting requirements in the US that further complicate the topic and specifically affects availability of resources. Donors are able to restrict how or when a nonprofit may use a particular contribution. These donor-restricted contributions can result in the recording of revenues (and subsequently result in a profit) even though the organization cannot spend the resources at all or as it wishes.

To illustrate, suppose a donor gives $20,000 to a nonprofit agency, and insists that the contribution be held in perpetuity. The nonprofit may invest the money and spend all or part of the income derived from the $20,000, but the $20,000 itself may not be spent. From the perspective of the organization, the $20,000 donation exists not to spend today, but to generate future revenues that fund future spending. However, in the year the donation is received, the nonprofit would record revenue (albeit restricted) of $20,000 in addition to any other surplus generated that year. Hence, when considering surpluses or profits in the nonprofit sector, the role of donor-imposed restrictions ought to be taken into account because not all profits are available for use as internal funds.

Further, some leftover funds should not be thought of as "slack." Some of these assets are held for working capital purposes, usually cash that is used for operational and transactional purposes; other assets may be held as operating reserves—liquid available cash (or near-cash such as money market accounts) held primarily for temporary emergencies or growth opportunities. These reserves need to have no donor restrictions attached to them because managers need to use operating reserves with some level of discretion. Sloan, Charles, and Kim (2016) note that managers may consider slack and reserves in other forms beyond liquid available resources as well. For example, managers might consider having an open line of credit (short-term unsecured borrowing capability) as a form of reserve account; investment accounts could serve a similar purpose because managers might liquidate assets relatively quickly when needed, or pledge the assets as collateral for borrowing. However, for our purposes, slack and reserves refer to relatively liquid and available assets that can be inexpensively deployed when needed.

Importantly, nonprofit governing boards may also designate accumulated surpluses as reserves or even as endowment. Calabrese and Ely (2017) note that about one-third of the total assets reported in endowments in the Form 990 Part D are technically free from donor restrictions. From a financial accounting perspective, these resources still lack donor restrictions and so they are considered "without donor restriction." Funds such as these are referred to as "quasi-endowments" and boards may access these funds in case of emergencies. However, if invested and commingled with donor-restricted assets, these quasi-endowments become subject to prudent investor policies that may make them difficult to access and use as reserves. In the case of operating reserves, earmarking these funds for emergency still makes them available because of the absence of explicit donor restrictions (Calabrese & Ely, 2017).

Hansmann (1990) discusses endowments in higher education, but his analysis is largely generalizable to other nonprofit organizations as well. He defines endowments as "large financial reserves." The term reserves in his analysis is not the same as "operating reserves" as Hansmann (1990, p. 3) differentiates between operating and endowment assets. Nevertheless, he does point out that quasi-endowment versus restricted endowment can be affected by solicitation practices (for example, adding some unrestricted donations to endowment might induce marginal donors to also give because they are drawn to the perpetuity of giving to endowment; hence, adding to quasi-endowment may be an effective fundraising strategy), as well as spending policies that determine whether earnings are accumulated or expended.

8.2   *Existing Literature*

As noted previously, some early theories about nonprofit behavior posited that their financial goal was breakeven, in which annual expenses and annual revenues were equal. Under this assumption, profits were assumed not to be a goal and simply the result of poor budgeting, shocks, or good fortunes. Any of these excess funds were expected to be used for the nonprofit's charitable output (Hansmann, 1980). Weisbrod (1988) was among the first to suggest that this assumption might be incorrect, that surpluses (revenues in excess of expenses) might provide utility to nonprofit managers. To some extent, actual practices of nonprofits reflect both of these views: a Nonprofit Finance Fund survey of nonprofit agencies found that 52 percent of agencies budgeted for breakeven financial operations, and 29 percent budgeted for an operating surplus (Nonprofit Finance Fund, 2018). However, one possibility is that more nonprofit agencies would prefer to plan for a surplus but are unable to. Sloan, Charles, and Kim (2016) find that managers are unable in many cases to find enough resources to earn profits and fund reserves. Another possibility is that nonprofit agencies might not want to reveal plans that include surpluses because managers want to obfuscate this goal to boards or other stakeholders. As noted earlier, nonprofit agencies that are perceived as hoarding resources rather than spending them on mission services might be subject to penalties from donors.

Tuckman and Chang (1992) were among the first to articulate that nonprofit managers might derive utility from profits and accumulating surpluses beyond simply providing future mission-related services. These reasons include:

1) Subsidizing clients unable to pay the full cost of the service (which arguably could be a mission-related goal for a nonprofit agency);
2) Providing capital for diversification into new areas;
3) Serving as a reserve fund;
4) Providing independence from donors; and
5) As a measure of success.

Tuckman and Chang's (1992) important contribution to this part of nonprofit finance is the explanation of why surpluses are purposeful and a potential goal for nonprofit agencies.

Building from this notion that surpluses were a goal of nonprofit managers, Calabrese (2012) hypothesized that agents actually sought surpluses free from donor restrictions (unrestricted profits). Further, while Tuckman and Chang (1992) implicitly assumed that any level of profits would be the goal, Calabrese (2012) finds that nonprofit agencies seek low levels of profits annually, perhaps to avoid appearing too wealthy. Nonprofits that seem to hold too much wealth might be deemed by some stakeholders (donors, insurance companies, etc.) as needing fewer future revenues which would hurt future financial conditions. Nevertheless, the existing literature finds evidence supportive of nonprofits seeking to earn annual surpluses, while avoiding reporting excessive amounts of accumulated resources, perhaps to avoid appearing not in need (Calabrese, 2011a). Hoarding of money might be viewed as reducing potential trust in the organization because donors expect charitable funds to be spent.

Even measuring surpluses and margins are difficult in the nonprofit sector. Measurement challenges stem, in large part, from the common use of administrative data via the IRS Form 990 to determine surpluses or margin, but also from the persistence of cash accounting in the nonprofit sector (Calabrese, 2011b). Bowman, Tuckman, and Young (2012) present five different measures of nonprofit surplus and are especially critical of the most commonly used calculation, which they refer to as "Surplus per Form 990." The difficulty in measuring even simple financial concepts because of data shortcomings as well as theoretical considerations (unrestricted versus restricted surpluses, for example) has no doubt limited testing and refining existing theories about nonprofit agencies' goals about surplus and margin.

Nevertheless, margin or surplus measured as revenue less expenses does provide an indicator of excess resources acquired by a nonprofit agency during the fiscal year. While no consensus exists on what this amount should be, Bowman (2011) articulates a "sustainability principle" in which annual surpluses are equal or greater than a return on assets matching the long-term inflation rate. Such a surplus ratio would permit nonprofits to replace and maintain their assets over the long-term.

In 2017, 59 percent of nonprofit agencies reported a surplus (measured as total revenues less expenses). The details are presented in Table 4. While the unconditional median surplus (that is, all observations and not just those organizations reporting a surplus) was a nominal 2.4 percent (meaning that nonprofit agencies kept as profit 2.4 cents of every dollar earned), this was only 1.4 percent when adjusted for inflation (which is similar to findings in Calabrese, 2012). This suggests that the average nonprofit agency was able to keep pace with rising costs. Different subsectors reveal variation in average margins. Human service nonprofits have the lowest margins, while those in education have the highest (also, this is the subsector with the most endowments that likely saw strong investment growth in 2017). Smaller nonprofit agencies report larger average margins, but this is likely just a reflection of small scale having large effects on the margin ratio. Older nonprofit agencies, defined as having a ruling date more than twenty years in the past, have lower margin ratios than newer nonprofit agencies. A nonprofit's ruling date indicates when the organization obtained formal recognition of its tax-exempt status from the IRS. This might reflect lifecycles in which younger nonprofits are earning more profits to invest in expansion, or higher expected uncertainty in future revenues which increases the demand for precautionary savings.

Margin also depends on where nonprofits earn their revenues. Surprisingly, more donative nonprofit agencies report higher median margin ratios than more commercial nonprofits that generate program service revenue. This is consistent with the findings of Duquette (2017), who finds nonprofits spend most revenues in the same year they are earned, suggesting low margins. However, Duquette (2017) also finds that nonprofits also have a tendency to save portions of private contributions for future consumption perhaps because future donations are more uncertain. Recall, though, that these donative organizations must report all donations even those with donor restrictions on the operating statement; hence, the higher margins here might simply reflect large donor-restricted donations that will be used not for services, but for generating future revenues.

The discussion thus far has focused on theories about why profits might be desirable, and data that reports the actual experience of nonprofit agencies

TABLE 4   Margins calculated from the Form 990 data, 2017

	Margin ratio (median)	Share with a positive margin (surplus)
All	2.4%	59.4%
Subsector (NTMAJ5)		
Arts, culture, and humanities	2.6%	58.3%
Education	3.6%	63.7%
Health	2.4%	60.7%
Human services	1.4%	56.7%
Other	3.6%	60.7%
Size (total expense percentile)		
<= 25th percentile	7.8%	62.0%
> 25th percentile, <= 75th percentile	1.7%	56.7%
> 75th percentile, <= 95th percentile	1.6%	60.6%
> 95th percentile	2.3%	67.5%
Organization Age		
Ruling Date (<= 20 years ago)	2.9%	59.8%
Ruling Date (> 20 years ago)	2.0%	59.2%
Revenue Dependence (> 50%)		
Contributions, Gifts, and Grants	3.1%	61.0%
Program Service Revenue	1.3%	56.7%

SOURCE: FROM CALABRESE AND ELY (2020). DERIVED FROM IRS EXEMPT
ORGANIZATIONS BUSINESS MASTER FILE EXTRACT (EO BMF) FY 2015–2017. THE MARGIN
RATIO REPORTS THE UNCONDITIONAL MEDIANS FOR THE ENTIRE SAMPLE, NOT JUST
ORGANIZATIONS WITH POSITIVE MARGINS.

(although no such data exists on voluntary associations). Another reason organizations might want to accumulate surpluses is to build operating reserves.
Many financial experts recommend three months' worth of reserves, equivalent to 25 percent of annual operating expenses, to protect an organization
from revenue shocks; however, there is no real magic to this number and this
rule of thumb has become mostly universally accepted despite lacking any
empirical basis. Blackwood and Pollak (2009) note that operating reserves are
an indicator of financial health, and found that 57 percent of their Washington,
DC sample had reserves that were less than three months' worth of expenses.
Their analysis found that older and larger nonprofits were more likely to have
the 25 percent of annual operating expense amount in reserve. Organizations

more dependent upon government support and self-generated program revenues reported less reserves than donative nonprofits. These results contradict
theory, which would speculate that self-generated revenue is easier to retain
than other revenue sources. At the same time, using funds received from
government support and contracts to fund reserves rather than provide the
associated service is actively discouraged and usually disallowed.

Using a similar definition of reserves as Blackwood and Pollak (2009),
Calabrese (2013) finds organizational size does not predict having reserves or
the size of reserves. Further, Calabrese (2013) finds that the revenue portfolio
of the organization influences reserve size, which differs from Blackwood and
Pollak's (2009) descriptive analysis: those more dependent upon government
funds hold less reserves, and donations are not a significant predictor. To the
extent that reserves are an indicator of financial health, these findings suggest that government funds may actually reduce the financial sustainability of
organizations. Nonprofits reporting permanently restricted true endowment
also report lower operating reserves, perhaps suggesting that revenues derived
from endowment reduce the demand for reserves. Further, concerns that
donors will withdraw future donations because of reserves is not supported. In
fact, the findings of Calabrese (2011a) in which donations are only affected by
extremely high levels of accumulated resources (measured in this case as net
assets) may be applicable to reserves as well.

Whether reserves might negatively affect other financial aspects of nonprofits is an interesting question. If reserves might have significant costs associated
with them, then nonprofit agencies might opt instead for other mechanisms
that serve similar purposes but have lower costs attached to them. This is the
primary notion behind a study by Sloan, Charles, and Kim (2016) in which they
interview nonprofit managers about reserves and substitutes directly rather
than relying exclusively on administrative data. While Blackwood and Pollak
(2009) and Calabrese (2013) reveal low levels of operating reserves, these
findings might be because managers rely on other tools rather than explicit
reserves. While reserves may reflect good business practices, Sloan, Charles,
and Kim (2016) point out that nonprofit organizations operate in a unique and
different space in which using sound business practices may not always be
possible. Current needs may supersede future potential needs, and nonprofits
as a result may have a difficult time accumulating surpluses and saving for the
future. Managers might instead rely on lines of credit, trade credit, investment
accounts, and secured borrowings rather than build up a traditional operating
reserve. Nevertheless, these substitutes for reserves help explain the lack of
reserves in the sector, and display management adaptation to the realities
of the sector.

The primary goal of reserves is help maintaining organizational spending during difficult economic times when revenues might fall short of needed spending. Reserves effectively help smooth consumption over business cycles. These resources stave off challenging service cuts during times when there might be an increased demand for public services. Tuckman and Chang (1991) define nonprofits as financially vulnerable if they cannot withstand a fiscal shock without scaling back programs. Calabrese (2018) analyzes whether reserves do in fact help stabilize spending by nonprofits during times of volatility. The results indicate that reserves help to make up for some of the lost revenues, but these reserves are deficient at low current levels. Critically, the three-month rule of thumb may be insufficient to stabilize nonprofit spending, as much of the volatility exceeds this level. Given the existing cultural taboo around nonprofits accumulating too much wealth and the necessity to appear "lean" (Mitchell, 2017), whether or not the sector can accumulate the resources necessary to build reserves that provide effective relief during times of economic volatility remains an open issue.

While the benefits of reserves and slack are well known and articulated, others have also pointed out the potential costs of excess resources. A body of literature exists that is concerned with nonprofits accumulating too much wealth. Milofsky and Blades (1991), for example, focus on health charities, and articulate concerns about the amount of assets accumulated and the lack of accountability these private organizations have in how these publicly subsidized resources are used. In the for-profit sector, excess resources can be returned to owners or investors. No such mechanism exists in the nonprofit sector to return unused or unneeded revenues to donors or providers (Core, Guay, & Verdi, 2006). Therefore, excesses must be spent immediately, or held to be spent in the future. Because the nondistribution constraint forbids claims on these resources, excess funds may sit indefinitely with the nonprofit organization. Core, Guay, and Verdi (2006) find that nonprofit agencies with excess cash balances do exhibit lower program spending and higher chief executive officer (CEO) and director compensation compared to nonprofit agencies with lower cash balances. Again, the implication is that too much cash leads to inefficiencies, even though increased overhead spending does not have anything to do with efficiency necessarily. In a similar vein, Frumkin and Keating (2010) find that CEO compensation is higher when nonprofits maintain excess profits rather than spending them. On the other hand, Calabrese and Gupta (2019) analyze these prior findings around the agency problems of significant cash balances in nonprofits; they find that the results are highly sensitive to model specification. Calabrese (2018) also finds no evidence of agency problems with respect to reserve accumulation in nonprofit agencies. In addition, Lee and

Woroncowicz (2019) find agency problems do not explain nonprofit cash holdings. Therefore, whether maintaining slack resources leads to organizations' agency problems is an area of nonprofit finance in need of additional research because of inconclusive results.

8.3   *Foundations*

Turning briefly to foundations, which exist to fund other nonprofit agencies, the question of "how much to give now and how much to save for future giving" remains one of the most important issues for these grantmaking organizations (Deep & Frumkin, 2001). Nonprofit foundations must decide how much to distribute currently and how much to distribute in the future to the sector (Cordes & Sansing, 2007). This question is similar to the general question of how much should nonprofit agencies spend and how much should they save for the future. Unlike regular operating nonprofits, private foundations are required to pay out a minimal amount of their non-charitable-use assets annually. This payout requirement, however, is not applicable to community foundations, operating foundations, or DAFs. Current law requires a 5 percent minimum distribution, but adjustments (from prior period overpayments and underpayments, for example) can make this 5 percent minimum a bit amorphous. Details on the mechanics of foundation distributions can be found in Renz (2012). The 5 percent distribution is an estimate of a long-term real (after inflation) rate of return on invested assets which would permit foundations to maintain the real value of the corpus of their investments even without additional donations.

While nonprofit agencies spend most of their resources (as evidenced by their slim margins), foundations fund these providers (Fernandez & Hager, 2014). Holtz-Eakin and Smith (2010) note that nonprofit foundations are capable of quick responses to crises affecting the nonprofit sector. One of the primary questions for nonprofit finance, however, is whether or not foundations view the legal minimum distribution instead as a maximum ceiling for annual giving. Sansing and Yetman (2006) find variation in foundation payouts, with growing foundations more likely to exceed minimal required payout rates. Sansing (2010) notes that payout rates seem to increase during bad economic times, meaning that economic forces, not public policies, may be the greater influence of such payouts. On the other hand, Deep and Frumkin (2006) find no relationship between payout rates and endowment returns, which suggests the public policy around legal minimum is what drives foundation payouts. Although examining universities with endowments and not foundations per se, Brown and colleagues (2014) find evidence that organizations hoard endowments during economic shocks, but do not increase payouts during positive shocks. Again, these organizations are not subject to the same laws as foundations, despite perhaps having similarities in their financial motivations. Therefore, the current literature on foundation payout behavior is muddled, with no clear consensus.

Sansing (2010) attributes the findings to the different samples used to test theory. While the sample of Deep and Frumkin (2001) consists of mostly large and older foundations from 1972 to 1996, the sample of Sansing and Yetman (2006) covers 1994–2000 and is balanced. Clearly both time periods had different experiences with the stock market and social demands on nonprofit agencies, all of which could affect payouts. The current state of research on whether foundations increase or decrease payouts during times of economic shock, therefore, is best described as inconclusive. Currently, the literature has competing findings which are difficult to compare given differences in data. Future research may wish to re-examine foundation payouts with better data, stronger methods, and a clearer understanding of what the minimum distribution required really means.

Recent research has also begun to examine how foundation investment practices have fared. Heutel and Zeckhauser (2014a) note that some nonprofits appear to invest more effectively than others, but research on why is limited. Heutel and Zeckhauser (2014b) find private foundations in particular tend to overperform relative to other nonprofit investment returns. Hooke, Yook, and Chu (2019) find that foundations attempts to replicate the Yale-style of endowment investments (that is, using actively managed funds and alternative investments) resulted in significant transaction costs that did not necessarily benefit the foundations—and by extension their nonprofit beneficiaries. Future research might address whether foundations are shifting investments towards social investments (those investments that might have low or negative financial returns but add social value) or whether they ought to increase holdings in these fields as a normative matter. Alternately, might foundations be investing more conservatively to better ensure funds exist in perpetuity? Should foundations consider other issues beyond just expected profits when investing in companies? Who determines which companies and priorities and why? Additionally, how widespread is the use of program-related investments (PRIs)? These are a form of financing in which foundations provide capital to grantees. Unlike traditional grants, however, PRIs are repaid to the foundation, usually at borrowing rates that are less than available from traditional lenders. PRIs qualify as part of a foundation's required payout, despite the fact that they are paid back to the foundation and generate future income which can then be invested or disbursed in the future. The point is that foundation investment practices remain relatively under researched. Given changing societal norms, this area seems fruitful for important and interesting research to help us understand the priorities of foundations more completely.

9   Capital Structure

Capital structure theories are outlined in this section, with unique nonprofit issues detailed as well. Literature on capital structure in nonprofits is discussed as well as types of financing available to nonprofits. Much of the section focuses on the cost of capital, a key component of how organizations finance their expansions and acquisitions.

9.1   *Overview*

Jegers (2018) notes that an intuitive interpretation of any firm's balance sheet is that it is a description of what it owns (its assets) and the funding sources used to acquire these possessions. Funding sources here are not the same concept as earlier introduced in the discussion about revenue portfolios or interactions. Those funding sources are concerned with routine revenues that all organizations earn to operate. Rather, the balance sheet is concerned with debt—enforceable and usually fixed obligations that must be repaid—and equity—the value of the firm after accounting for debts. Capital structure, then, focuses on how organizations combine debt and equity to finance operations and expansion, and is oftentimes more focused on the long term—whereas the previous discussion about slack, margins, and working capital is more focused on the short term.

The fundamental accounting equation is written as:

Assets = Liabilities + Equity

This equation (which also reflects the information found on any balance sheet) reveals that all assets—that is, those which are owned by an organization—must be financed by either borrowing money from lenders (liabilities) or from those resources owned outright by the organization (equity). While liabilities are often thought of as coming from outsiders and equity from insiders, the reality is more complicated.

Why, though, is capital structure such an important issue for organizations? To continue with the above equation, consider that an organization wants to purchase some asset—perhaps a building, land, etc. To finance this purchase, the organization must come up with some mix of debt and equity (the right-hand side of the equation). In theory, the organization wants to find the mix of debt and equity that minimizes the costs to the organization. For entities that pay corporate income taxes, the cost of debt—interest—reduces operating profits, thereby lowering required tax payments; that is, there are tax benefits from using debt. Nonprofits do not pay corporate income taxes and so the cost of debt is simply the unadjusted interest cost. The cost of equity in nonprofits is more difficult to estimate but is the minimum rate of return necessary to attract capital to the investment (Heshmat, 1992). For any project, then, the cost of capital is the required rate of return on an investment of similar risk.

Why does the mix of funding matter? If an organization relies too heavily on debt, the cost of borrowing increases as lenders demand more compensation for the increased risk. In the for-profit sector, the cost of equity is almost always greater than the cost of debt, so there is an incentive to not rely excessively on equity as well. If the project cost of capital exceeds the required rate of return of similar investments of similar risk, the organization may fail to attract the necessary funding and miss the opportunity. However, the mix and cost of funding for nonprofits differs from for-profits. The mix of debt and equity in the nonprofit sector is more complicated, and the extant literature on nonprofit capital structure tries to tease out how these differences affect the cost of capital for such organizations.

There are several issues that further complicate the capital structure of nonprofits. Unlike in for-profit entities, the nondistribution constraint keeps profits earned by a nonprofit organization from being distributed to owners, so these profits become a source of funds for financing needs. These retained earnings may best be considered an internal source of equity. The other major source of equity in the nonprofit context comes from donations and gifts. These may best be considered an external source of equity. Unlike in the for-profit sector where investment capital is not recorded on the operating statement, all donations regardless of type (restricted or not) do flow through the operating statement for nonprofits (net of fundraising expenses because these expenses naturally reduce net assets). The result is that large capital infusions from donors can result in sizable reported surpluses in some years even though these donations might be intended for particular purposes. Paid-in capital in the for-profit sector (that is, funds raised by a business through selling equity) is a balance sheet account only because it is not a revenue earned from business operations, and as such does not affect operating statement accounts. Therefore, whereas equity infusions affect the operating statement of nonprofits, they do not always do so in for-profits. Regardless, these net assets (the nonprofit equivalent of "equity" on the balance sheet) serve as a source of funds that nonprofits might use to finance assets.

Some research speculates that nonprofits' cost of equity is always lower than their cost of debt, which is very different from for-profit entities (Jegers, 2018; Sloan et al., 1988). Even so, nonprofits face "equity constraints" in which available equity tends to fall short of funding needs (Gentry, 2002; Hansmann, 1981). As noted earlier, Hansmann (1981) argues that exempting nonprofits from corporate taxation helps alleviate (but not totally overcome) this problem because equity is therefore retained and not taxed away.

Debt is the other source of financing for assets. Borrowed money permits the organization to better match the costs of the assets with its benefits over longer time periods. Unlike using net assets, debt must be paid back to the lender with interest. In the case of financial debt, in which an organization borrows money from a financial institution such as a bank, the use of debt also introduces an additional stakeholder who monitors the financial performance of the borrower. Jegers (2003) develops a theoretical model that demonstrates that debt can help nonprofits maximize programmatic growth.

Nonprofits have access to various debt instruments. Importantly, nonprofits may borrow using tax-exempt debt. These are long-term borrowings issued through governments or public authorities in which investors do not pay income taxes on the interest received from owning the debt. As a result, the borrowing rate on tax-exempt debt in general is less than the borrowing rate on taxable debt. Recall that taxable organizations that borrow receive a tax advantage from borrowing because the interest cost reduces profits and, as a result, tax liabilities. Tax-exempt debt effectively equalizes the cost of debt for nonprofit entities because the cost is also "after tax"—just to the investor instead of the organization itself. For purposes of capital structure, the important point is that tax-exempt debt reduces the cost of borrowing for the nonprofit, which reduces the project cost of capital, and makes investing in a project less expensive. Tax-exempt borrowing by nonprofits has significantly grown over time, increasing about 8 percent annually in real terms since the late 1990s (Calabrese & Ely, 2016). Nonprofits that use tax-exempt debt must access the market through a conduit—usually a government agency or a public authority (Ely & Calabrese, 2017). Wedig, Hassan, and Morrisey (1996) find evidence that access to tax-exempt debt leads nonprofit agencies below optimal debt levels to issue more tax-exempt debt even when cash is sufficient to finance capital needs, because the lower cost/tax advantage provides an indirect arbitrage opportunity for the nonprofits. Wedig, Hassan, and Morrisey's (1996) primary contribution is to show that this incentive exists from the existence of tax arbitrage via tax-exempt borrowing. Ely and Calabrese (2017) find evidence that having to use these public conduits itself alters the structure of tax-exempt debt issued by nonprofit agencies. Specifically, conduits earn money when nonprofits issue debt, but also from annual fees paid by

TABLE 5   Comparison of capital structure measures and data over time

Measure	Calabrese (2011c): 1998–2003 data	IRS 2017 extract
Debt to asset ratio	0.40	0.29
	(0.50)	(0.55)
Financial debt to asset ratio	0.15	0.10
	(0.30)	(0.25)
Percent with financial debt outstanding	0.37	0.25

SOURCE: AUTHOR'S CALCULATIONS. DERIVED FROM IRS EXEMPT ORGANIZATIONS
BUSINESS MASTER FILE EXTRACT (EO BMF) FY 2017 AND FROM NCCS DIGITIZED DATA,
FY 1998–2003.

the nonprofit to the conduit as long as the tax-exempt debt remains outstanding. As a result, Ely and Calabrese (2017) find that tax-exempt debt issued by nonprofit agencies tends to have longer maturities than other debt. Hence, tax-exempt debt may induce more borrowing as Wedig, Hassan, and Morrisey (1996) find, and this debt may remain outstanding for longer periods of time as well (Ely & Calabrese, 2017).

Using the NCCS Digitized Data based on Form 990 data for 1998–2003, Calabrese (2011c) reports that the mean debt-to-asset ratio, the most common measure of capital structure in the literature, was 40 percent. This means that the average nonprofit agency in the sample financed about 40 percent of its assets with debt and 60 percent with net assets/equity. Using recent IRS data extracts from 2017, the mean debt to asset ratio is approximately 29 percent; this would suggest a decline in the use of debt over the past several decades and an increasing reliance upon equity (profits and donations). Further, when Calabrese (2011c) reported financial leverage ratios which only include tax-exempt borrowing and mortgages borrowed from banks in the numerator (with total assets as the denominator), the mean ratio drops to 15 percent. With the more recent IRS extracts, this mean ratio is only 10 percent. While Calabrese (2011c) reports 37 percent of the sample having financial debt outstanding, only 25 percent of the organizations reporting in 2017 have financial debt outstanding. Whether these changes reflect less actual borrowing by nonprofit agencies or changes in the sample used in the data are difficult to determine. In either case, this would suggest additional empirical research is needed not only to test capital structure theories, but also to address sampling concerns. In both cases, the data are limited to 501(c)3 organizations only. Table 5 summarizes these two analyses.

9.2   *Current Literature*

In both the for-profit and nonprofit literatures, two dominant capital structure theories exist. Both focus on the idea that an organization's cost of capital is a function of its mix of debt and equity outstanding. A for-profit firm that can lower its organizational cost of capital increases the present value of its future cash flows (that is, its current market value), so for-profit organizations have an incentive to find the mix of debt and equity that minimizes its cost of capital. For a nonprofit organization, lowering its cost of capital reduces its financing costs which, all else equal, leaves more resources for other organizational goals (whatever these might be).

The first is the static trade-off theory. This theory states that organizations determine an optimal amount of debt to have based on the costs and benefits of this debt. An organization that is more profitable may increase leverage more readily and easily than an organization that is less profitable. This theory predicts increased debt levels with increased profitability. The benefits of debt include reduced tax liabilities because the interest cost of debt reduces annual operating profits—thereby lowering taxes owed by the entity. Unlike for-profits, taxes have no significant effect on capital structure for nonprofits, however, because of tax exemption. Denison (2009), though, notes that nonprofits do pay taxes on unrelated business income, so nonprofits with this type of income may have an incentive to borrow to reduce taxes owed on this income. Omer and Yetman (2003) note that nonprofits shift expenses to taxable activities from exempt activities to reduce tax liabilities. Wedig, Hassan, and Morrisey (1996) and Gentry (2002) are two significant and important studies that find evidence of the static trade-off theory in the nonprofit sector; however, both of these analyses are limited to hospitals.

Debt is also thought to create a mechanism by which the agency problems associated with free cash flows are reduced. Hansmann (1990) suggests that nonprofit managers have incentives to build up endowments which generate free cash to ensure private benefits (such as better job security, better work environments, etc.). Fisman and Hubbard (2005) find evidence that executive compensation increases as donations increase for nonprofits in weak governance states, implying that managers divert resources for their own benefit. Core, Guay, and Verdi (2006) further find evidence that excessive endowment accumulation leads to increases in CEO compensation in nonprofits. Debt, then, might serve to absorb these free cash flows and reduce these potential agency problems. But adding debt adds costs. The most significant cost of debt comes in the form of financial distress to the borrower. Debt service must be paid, even at the expense of other activities such as programs. As detailed by Calabrese (2011c), financial distress costs to nonprofits include increased interest rates (borrowing costs) on debt, lack of access to the credit markets so that profitable investments are missed, asset sales, legal fees, and potentially loss of future donors who do not want to give to failing public charities. Other costs include the transaction costs from issuing debt or assuming a liability.

The other popular capital structure theory is the pecking order theory. In contrast to the static trade-off theory, the pecking order theory presumes that more profitable organizations are less likely to use debt than less profitable ones. Rather, internal equity sources (such as retained earnings) are the preferred financing source for management. Leverage decisions are presumed to be driven by information asymmetry in which external stakeholders view equity issues negatively because it dilutes the ownership of the current investors; as a result, retained earnings are preferred, then debt, and then stock issuance. Hence, the theory predicts an inverse relationship with fiscal health and debt.

Nonprofit "equity" is arguably more complicated than equity in the for-profit sector, and needs further elaboration in capital structure theory. Donors may restrict contributions for specific purposes or in perpetuity. Hence, only net assets without donor restrictions may be directed by managers as a financing source in nonprofits. Nonprofit managers may have a preference for internal capital because of aversion to financial distress. While managers might not suffer pecuniary losses from a distressed organization, they might fear reputational costs (Bowman, 2002), leading them to favor internal retained earnings compared to debt. Donors who provide significant gifts to nonprofit agencies may exercise some oversight about how the organization operates; Denison (2009) notes that a donor willing to finance a capital campaign—large multiyear campaigns frequently undertaken by nonprofits to construct buildings or acquire properties—may help organizations avoid the debt markets altogether. Pecking order theory, overall, posits that nonprofits do not have a target level of debt, and instead prefer internal sources of capital (such as accumulated unrestricted profits) to borrowing.

Bowman (2007) further notes that endowment complicates the study of nonprofit capital structure. Endowments are assets intended to produce income for a nonprofit; hence, they serve as part of the capital structure of the organization (assets) as well as part of its revenue generation (Bowman, 2007). Donors may prefer to give to an endowment because it helps ensure the long-term viability of the nonprofit agency (Bowman, Keating, & Hager, 2007; Hansmann, 1990). Hansmann (1990) posits that alumni of universities have an incentive to donate to already-wealthy institutions to help ensure that they remain financially viable long after the individuals consume services; a university that ceases operations might tarnish alumni reputations. Bowman

(2002) treats endowed nonprofits as service-producing operating entities and customized mutual funds generating investment income. That is, Bowman (2002) suggests that separating endowment from the rest of the organization permits better insight into its financing decisions. Bowman (2002) finds that endowed and unendowed nonprofit agencies reveal different capital structure preferences—endowed entities behave in manners consistent with the static trade-off theory, while unendowed entities behave in manners consistent with the pecking order theory. This finding is supported by Calabrese (2011c) who isolates those assets without donor restrictions (used as a proxy for the nonprofit agency without any endowment) and finds evidence of the pecking order theory. In an international context, Garcia-Rodriguez and Jegers (2017) find that nongovernmental organizations (NGOs) in different European countries issue different amounts of debt depending on their locations. NGOs in the United Kingdom issued much less debt compared to those in Spain and in Belgium. Despite the differences in the use of debt, NGOs did reveal behavior consistent with the pecking order theory.

One reason the extant literature is less developed in this regard is that endowment data were not readily available until recently. The Form 990 did not require disclosure about endowments until 2008. Prior to this, researchers interested in the topic had to devise methods to estimate endowments: Bowman (2002) used investment assets; Gentry (2002) and Fisman and Hubbard (2005) used total net assets; Core, Guay, and Verdi (2006) used the asset accounts "cash plus savings plus investments," as well as unrestricted net assets; Calabrese (2011c) and Calabrese (2013) used permanently restricted net assets; and Bowman, Tuckman, and Young (2012) inferred an endowment when investments (assets) exceeded annual expenses. Different definitions captured different aspects of endowment, but none were consistent and limited the development of this particular area of nonprofit finance. Calabrese and Ely (2017) used new data reported on the Form 990 and determine that endowments are concentrated in higher education nonprofit agencies (over 60 percent of total sector endowment assets), and income generated from endowments cover on average over 4 percent of total expenses. However, the sector's heterogeneity is evident in endowment data as well. Investment earnings are far more important to higher education and arts nonprofit agencies—averaging 8 to 10 percent of expenses—compared to human service agencies—averaging just 2 percent of expenses. Nevertheless, future research on capital structure in nonprofit agencies will no doubt benefit from better data on endowments that will permit researchers to more accurately measure endowment and separate it from routine operations.

Another issue with this line of research is that much of the early nonprofit capital structure analyses focused exclusively on nonprofit hospitals. Important papers that fit this description include Bacon (1992), Gentry (2002), and Wedig and colleagues (1988, 1996). Most find evidence of static trade-off theory, with debt targeting and adjustments over time. Hospitals are unique nonprofit agencies, though. They tend to be capital-intensive, generate exchange revenue from patients, and are financially sophisticated. Importantly, nonprofit hospitals never faced limits on tax-exempt debt issuances, while other nonprofit agencies did. Following the Tax Reform Act of 1986, non-hospital nonprofits were limited to $150 million of tax-exempt debt outstanding; those in excess of this amount could not issue additional tax-exempt debt, and those below had to ration their capacity to issue. Hence, beginning in 1987, non-hospital nonprofits faced a different financing landscape than hospitals: whereas hospitals could issue as much tax-exempt debt as they could, other nonprofits were limited significantly. Ely and Calabrese (2016) show that when this cap on tax-exempt borrowing was unexpectedly lifted in 1997, non-hospital nonprofit agencies began issuing more tax-exempt debt because of an effective reduction in the cost of capital for nonprofit agencies. What the literature does not explore, however, is whether nonprofit hospitals paid lower tax-exempt bond yields because of less competition for investors and whether this changed after 1997 when new issuers suddenly entered the market and competed with hospitals.

Also recall that both Bowman (2002) and Calabrese (2011c) find evidence of the pecking order theory in nonprofits when endowment is separated. Jegers and Verschueren (2006) similarly find behavior consistent with pecking order behavior. These findings are in contrast to most of the earlier analyses that focused on hospitals. One potential issue is that access to the tax-exempt debt markets for non-hospital nonprofits was, as we have seen, limited in 1987 and then removed in 1997. Research has not examined whether these changes permitting unconstrained tax-exempt borrowing also altered the behavior of nonprofit agencies. The data used in Bowman (2002) are from when nonprofits were constrained in their tax-exempt debt issuances, which might naturally lead to finding behavior consistent with pecking theory (that is, equity preference over debt); Calabrese (2011c) uses data immediately following the removal of the constraint when nonprofits may still have been adjusting to having no tax-exempt debt limits. In other words, both studies find behavior consistent with pecking order theory, but these findings might reflect the existence of a public policy that no longer exists. Hence, future research might investigate if removing this cap on tax-exempt borrowing for all nonprofits reveals different behavior than that which current research has found to date.

Another consideration is whether standard capital structure theories adopted from the corporate literature are suited to predict nonprofit behavior and decision. Alternately, does future research need to develop theories that incorporate unique nonprofit characteristic? For example, while Calabrese (2011c) finds evidence consistent with the pecking order theory, he also finds evidence that nonprofits do seem to slowly adjust their debt levels over time, which is actually inconsistent with the pecking order theory and is more consistent with the findings in Wedig and colleagues (1996)—both of whom used partial adjustment models to test the notion of adjustment over time. Pecking order theory (at least in its strictest sense) predicts that debt targets do not exist within organizations, that funding is simply a matter of priority (cheapest internal first, then more expensive internal, then external). This slow adjustment would run counter to this interpretation of pecking order because it suggests that nonprofits do have some weak debt target after all. Calabrese (2011c) explains this seemingly contradictory finding that nonprofit agencies may make financing decisions on probable future resources as well as current resources. Keeping internal financial resources available in the future may lead some nonprofit managers to issue debt rather than using up all their equity first. Further, if there was a capital constraint (as in pre-1997 for most of the sector), this might suggest organizations using up small portions of the tax-exempt debt-issuing capacity. Further research might examine whether this significant federal policy reversal changes nonprofit capital structure behavior as well.

A final consideration is that none of the capital structure analyses consider off-balance-sheet liabilities. Theoretically, whether debt is included on the balance sheet or not should not be germane; debt is debt. Off-balance-sheet liabilities may seem to managers as having less expensive costs of capital than on-balance-sheet debt, and this might explain the appeal in part. One problem is that off-balance-sheet debt is difficult to observe and include in analyses. Because capital structure theory and analysis use reported balance sheet liabilities as the starting point for understanding costs of capital, liabilities that are excluded from the balance sheet likely reduce the assumed cost of capital—because the cost of capital is generally increasing with levels of liabilities. A natural concern, then, is that excluding these liabilities makes a nonprofit appear more financially healthy than it truly is.

The most prominent off-balance-sheet liability is unfunded pension liabilities. While these may seem unimportant to nonprofit agencies, Calabrese and Searing (2019) document that organizations with defined benefit pension plans do carry significant off-balance-sheet unfunded liabilities. Such data are not included in the Form 990, but are available in the Department of Labor's

Form 5500, which pension plan sponsors must file. Calabrese and Searing (2019) find over 2,000 nonprofit agencies have pension systems, with the majority being sponsored by health care organizations. These systems cover a large number of nonprofit employees—between 15 and 21 percent of the estimated total nonprofit workforce in the US. The extent to which these liabilities influence the decision to issue debt or use equity is untested. However, Calabrese and Searing (2019) demonstrate that managing pension contributions (for consumption smoothing or earnings management) is common in the sector. By extension, it seems that these liabilities might influence the financing decisions of nonprofit agencies, but no literature exists. Nor do we know if these pension liabilities influence capital development of nonprofit agencies. The corporate for-profit literature has demonstrated the role of these pension liabilities on debt issuance and capital formation, and yet the effect of pension liabilities on nonprofit finances is relatively unknown.

9.3   *Capital Budgeting*

Capital structure theory and research focuses on the funding of investments, typically large and long-lived assets. Empirical work, although incomplete, has attempted to understand the financing decisions of nonprofits. Virtually no research considers how nonprofits arrive at which investment to choose in the first place. Stated differently, the process of capital budgeting in nonprofit organizations remains relatively unexplored. Capital budgeting is a process by which each potential investment or project is evaluated to determine the long-term economic and financial returns to the organizations. The financing of these chosen investments is what necessitates debt and equity. In some sense, the study of capital structure has examined the cart without really considering the horse.

Undoubtedly, great variation must exist in capital budgeting practices throughout the nonprofit sector. While Zietlow (1989) found that less than 15 percent of survey respondents in religious nonprofits even attempted to analyze capital investments, Reiter and colleagues (2000) find evidence that nonprofit hospitals tend to use accepted capital budgeting techniques such as net present values, internal rates of return, and payback methods. Further, the use of these techniques has seemingly increased throughout the health care sector and become increasingly sophisticated (see, for example, Kocher, 2007, for a review of past surveys of health care organizations). The sector, therefore, likely has significant variation in capital budgeting practices.

Capital budgeting in the nonprofit context, however, might not just be a simple traditional comparison of the financial costs and benefits of a particular investment. As noted by Young and colleagues (2019), the cost benefit analysis framework used for capital budgeting can be useful for evaluating public action that provides public good (traditionally accomplished through governments); however, the same framework can be applied to decide on investments by private actors that provide public goods (through nonprofits or social enterprises). These cost-benefit analyses in the nonprofit and social enterprise arenas include not just financial benefits, but also social benefits to parties external to the organization. In addition to this double bottom-line, some now include a triple bottom-line and consider environmental benefits as well (Young et al., 2019). Estimating benefits in these conditions are oftentimes difficult to identify, estimate, and measure. Yet surely at least some nonprofit organizations must engage in these analyses.

Undoubtedly the lack of research on capital budgeting—and nonprofit operating budgeting in general—likely derives from the difficulty in obtaining meaningful data on the topic. Unlike regulatory filings, budgets are entirely internal documents that need not be disclosed to the public. Yet, understanding the calculus of investment decisions—from what techniques are used, to how discount rates are estimated, to how future costs and benefits are forecasted and estimated, to how investments are chosen in an environment plagued by funding constraints—seems critical to understand the capital funding decisions of nonprofits.

10   Discussion and Conclusion

Research on nonprofit finance has certainly grown in quantity and quality over the past few decades. Articles are published across disciplines and across fields, using various theoretical frameworks and increasingly sophisticated methods. A summary of important takeaways from the current state of the literature is outlined here.

The nonprofit sector is extraordinarily heterogeneous. While this is hardly a surprise to those who study or engage with the sector, it needs acknowledgment. Some nonprofits are small voluntary organic organizations, such as grassroots associations (Smith, 2000), that basically raise and spend the same amount of money each year for the benefit of members. Others are large sophisticated bureaucracies, usually nonprofit agencies, dedicated to addressing commonplace needs (private and public). Still others address niche needs for specific populations. Theories that attempt to explain such a diverse and heterogeneous group of organizations are bound to fail.

The heterogeneity of the sector is also reflected in the revenue portfolios of nonprofit organizations, mainly nonprofit agencies as reviewed here (Smith,

2017). Portfolio theory has explained how nonprofits might mitigate the risks inherent in certain revenue streams and construct optimum portfolios. Benefit theory has more recently tried to identify optimal revenue streams for a nonprofit organization based on who benefits from the service provided. Regardless of theory, researchers have studied whether different revenue streams interact with each other; that is, do some revenue streams cause other revenue streams to increase or decrease? One of the most common examinations of revenue interactions is the effect of government funding on private contributions. The research remains unsettled, but the results increasingly appear immaterial. Donating to nonprofits (whether money or time) may not be a strictly rational or logical calculus as the basic models assume. Instead, individuals often donate and volunteer based on other motivations. Whether commercial revenues crowd-out donations also remains a research area with unsettled results.

On the uses of funds, nonprofits face incentives to direct money towards program services rather than overhead. Alternately, nonprofits may manipulate financial disclosures to make program spending ratios appear more favorable to them than they truly are. Nonprofits face these incentives because few if any performance measures exist that allow donors and other stakeholders to evaluate the outcomes of the organization. Researchers have warned against relying upon these measures for decades. Lacking these metrics, nonprofits are held to be fiscally trustworthy by meeting cost ratios or program-spending ratios that have no real relationship to effectiveness or efficiency. One potential solution to this problem is to encourage the development of outcome measures that begins identifying nonprofit agencies that provide services efficiently and effectively relative to their peers.

Another second-order effect from the focus on trustworthiness is that nonprofit agencies in general have a difficult time implementing and maintaining financial tools that would make business operations run more smoothly and at lower cost. For example, rather than devoting so much spending to current services, nonprofit agencies might be able to build and maintain reserve accounts, perhaps even financed with routine operating surpluses, so that routine business cycles can be managed without significant and unplanned service cutbacks. But the current nonprofit ecosystem may make it difficult for organizations in general to generate surpluses sufficient to maintain purchasing power, maintain adequate working capital and liquidity needs, and save for the future.

Similarly, the debt markets, while much more accessible than in the past, are used primarily by large and wealthy nonprofit agencies almost exclusively. This is in part because of the costs of issuing tax-exempt debt and the subsequent administrative tasks associated with such debt. But it also reflects a stubborn norm that many nonprofits will not assume debt even for proper purposes such as capital investment because of the fear that debt will lead to financial distress. Debt might actually be more valuable to nonprofit agencies in the start-up phase, when capital is difficult to acquire, especially since no equity market exists. Further, funders' insistence on funding current service provision rather than past debts make it more difficult in general for nonprofits to service debt. This is likely why nonprofit agencies on average prefer equity capital from surpluses, capital campaigns, and the like to fund capital needs. However, as noted earlier, generating sufficient equity remains problematic in the nonprofit sector.

Finally, despite the advent of "big data," nonprofit scholars still lack data that are sufficient to meet research needs. Much of financial theory remains rudimentary or unsettled because the data needed to rigorously and empirically test theories is elusive. Form 990 is the only source of data on many nonprofit agencies' finances. Yet the majority of organizations do not even file the Form 990, nor does the form even comport with GAAP or the entity concept (that is, rather than reporting on a nonprofit and its legal entities in a consolidated format as in financial statements, the Form 990 reports each legal entity as a separate and independent entity). While scholars have become creative about data sources and even begun to run experiments, the research community would benefit from administrative data that are better suited to answer the questions scholars want to pursue. While the IRS routinely solicits suggestions on Form 990 changes from the nonprofit community, researchers need to create a more vocal presence to inform what data are created in the first place.

Acknowledgements

I thank Richard Steinberg for providing extraordinary feedback on drafts of this article. His patience and attention to detail have greatly improved it, and I owe him a debt of gratitude. I also wish to thank David Horton Smith for his encouragement during the planning and writing process.

Author Biography

Thad D. Calabrese, PhD, is associate professor of public and nonprofit financial management at the Robert F. Wagner Graduate School of Public Service at New York University, and is director of the school's finance specialization. His research focuses on nonprofit and government accounting and finance and is published in the Journal of Public Administration Research and Theory (JPART), Public Administration Review, Public Budgeting & Finance (PBF), Journal of Accounting and Public Policy, Nonprofit and Voluntary Sector Quarterly, National Tax Journal, Public Finance Review, and Nonprofit Management & Leadership (NML), among others. He currently serves on the editorial board of NML, PBF, and JPART. He has served on the Association for Budgeting and Financial Management's member-elected executive committee and currently is the chair. In addition, he serves on the Governmental Accounting Standards Advisory Council. Thad also currently serves as treasurer of the Association for Research on Nonprofit Organizations and Voluntary Action. Prior to entering academia, he worked as a financial manager in the nonprofit sector and in local government.

Bibliography

Andreoni, J. (1990). Impure altruism and donations to public goods: A theory of warm-glow giving. *Economic Journal, 100*(June), 467–477.

Andreoni, J. (1998). Toward a theory of charitable fund-raising. *Journal of Political Economy, 106*(6), 1186–1213.

Andreoni, J. (2006). Leadership giving in charitable fund-raising. *Journal of Public Economic Theory, 8*(1), 1–22.

Andreoni, J. & Payne, A. A. (2011a). Is crowding out due entirely to fundraising? Evidence from a panel of charities. *Journal of Public Economics, 95*(5–6), 334–343.

Andreoni, J. & Payne, A. A. (2011b). Crowding-out charitable contributions in Canada: New knowledge from the north (No. w17635). National Bureau of Economic Research.

Andreoni, J., Harbaugh, W. T., & Vesterlund, L. (2008). Altruism in experiments. In S. N. Durlauf & L. E. Blume (Eds.) *The new Palgrave dictionary of economics: Volume 1–8* (pp. 134–138) London: Palgrave Macmillan.

Anthony, R. N., Dearden, J., & Bedford, N. M. (1984). *Management control systems.* Homewood, IL: Richard D. Irwin.

Arrow, K. J. (1963). Uncertainty and the welfare economics of medical care. *American Economic Review, 53*, 941–973.

Arrow, K. J. (1974). Gifts and exchanges. *Philosophy & Public Affairs, 1*, 343–362.

Baber, W. R., Daniel, P. L., & Roberts, A. A. (2002). Compensation to managers of charitable organizations: An empirical study of the role of accounting measures of program activities. *The Accounting Review, 77*(3), 679–693.

Bacon, P. W. (1992). Do capital structure theories apply to nonprofit hospitals? *Journal of the Midwest Finance Association, 21*(1), 86–90.

Becker, G. S. (1974). A theory of social interactions. *Journal of Political Economy, 82*(6), 1063–1093.

Bekkers, R. & Bowman, W. (2009). The relationship between confidence in charitable organizations and volunteering revisited. *Nonprofit and Voluntary Sector Quarterly, 38*(5), 884–897.

Bekkers, R. & Wiepking, P. (2011). A literature review of empirical studies of philanthropy: Eight mechanisms that drive charitable giving. *Nonprofit and Voluntary Sector Quarterly, 40*(5), 924–973.

Bielefeld, W. (1992). Nonprofit funding environment relations: Theory and application. *Voluntas, 3*, 48–70.

Blackwood, A. S. & Pollak, T. H. (2009). Washington-area nonprofit operating reserves. The Urban Institute, No. 20. Available at: http://webarchive.urban.org/uploaded pdf/411913_dc_nonprofit_reserves.pdf.

Borgonovi, F. (2006). Do public grants to American theatres crowd-out private donations? *Public Choice, 126*(3–4), 429–451.

Bowman, H. W. (2002). The uniqueness of nonprofit finance and the decision to borrow. *Nonprofit Management & Leadership, 12*(3), 292–311.

Bowman, H. W. (2007). Managing endowment and other assets. In D. R. Young (Ed.), *Financing nonprofits: Putting theory into practice* (pp. 271–289). Lanham, MD: AltaMira Press.

Bowman, H. W. (2011). The nonprofit difference. *Nonprofit Quarterly*, May 9. Available at: https://nonprofitquarterly.org/2011/05/09/the-nonprofit-difference/.

Bowman, H. W. (2017). Toward a theory of membership association finance. *Nonprofit and Voluntary Sector Quarterly, 46*(4), 772–793.

Bowman, H. W., Keating, E., & Hager, M. (2007). Investment income. In D. R. Young (Ed.), *Financing nonprofits: Putting theory into practice* (pp. 157–181). Lanham, MD: AltaMira Press.

Bowman, H. W., Tuckman, H. P., & Young, D. R. (2012). Issues in nonprofit finance research: Surplus, endowment, and endowment portfolios. *Nonprofit and Voluntary Sector Quarterly, 41*, 560–579.

Brooks, A. C. (2000). Is there a dark side to government support for nonprofits? *Public Administration Review, 60*(3), 211–218.

Brown, J. R., Dimmock, S. G., Kang, J., & Weisbrenner, S. J. (2014). How university endowments respond to financial market shocks: Evidence and implications. *American Economic Review, 104*(3), 931–962.

Buchheit, S. & Parsons, L. M. (2006). An experimental investigation of accounting information's influence on the individual giving process. *Journal of Accounting and Public Policy, 25*(6), 666–686.

Calabrese, T. D. (2011a). Do donors penalize nonprofit organizations with accumulated wealth? *Public Administration Review, 71*(6), 859–869.

Calabrese, T. D. (2011b). Public mandates, market monitoring, and nonprofit financial disclosures. *Journal of Accounting and Public Policy 30*(1), 71–88.

Calabrese, T. D. (2011c). Testing competing capital structure theories of nonprofit organizations. *Public Budgeting & Finance, 31*(3), 119–143.

Calabrese, T. D. (2012). The accumulation of nonprofit profits: A dynamic analysis. *Nonprofit and Voluntary Sector Quarterly, 41*(2), 300–324.

Calabrese, T. D. (2013). Running on empty: The operating reserves of U.S. nonprofit organizations. *Nonprofit Management & Leadership, 23*(3), 281–302.

Calabrese, T. D. (2018). Do operating reserves stabilize spending by nonprofit organizations? *Nonprofit Management & Leadership, 28*(3), 295–301.

Calabrese, T. D. & Ely, T. L. (2016). Borrowing for the public good: The growing importance of tax-exempt bonds for public charities. *Nonprofit and Voluntary Sector Quarterly, 45*(3), 458–477.

Calabrese, T. D. & Ely, T. L. (2017). Understanding and measuring endowment in public charities. *Nonprofit and Voluntary Sector Quarterly, 46*(4), 859–873.

Calabrese, T. D. & Ely, T. L. (2020). Reserves, margin, and slack. In I. Garcia-Rodriguez and M. E. Romero-Merino (Eds.), *Financing non-profit organizations* (pp. 114–128). New York: Routledge.

Calabrese, T. D. & Gupta, A. (2019). A replication of "agency problems of excess endowment holdings in not-for-profit firms" (Journal of Accounting and Economics). *Public Finance Review, 47*(4), 747–774.

Calabrese, T. D. & Searing, E. A. (2019). The strategic use of pensions by not-for-profit organizations. *Journal of Pension Economics & Finance, 18*(3), 388–414.

Callen, J. L. (1994). Money donations, volunteering and organizational efficiency. *The Journal of Productivity Analysis, 5*, 215–228.

Cantor, A. (2018). Key questions about donor-advised funds ignored in study. *The Chronicle of Philanthropy*, March 12. Available at: https://www.philanthropy.com /article/Opinion-Key-Questions-About/242794.

Carroll, D. A. & Stater, K. J. (2009). Revenue diversification in nonprofit organizations: Does it lead to financial stability? *Journal of Public Administration Research and Theory, 19*(4), 947–966.

Chang, C. F. & Tuckman, H. P. (1990). Why do nonprofit managers accumulate surpluses, and how much do they accumulate? *Nonprofit Management & Leadership, 1*(2), 117–135.

Chang, C. F. & Tuckman, H. P. (1991). Financial vulnerability and attrition as measures of non-profit performance. *Annals of Public and Cooperative Economics, 62*(4), 655–672.

Chang, C. F. & Tuckman, H. P. (1994). Revenue diversification among non-profits. *Voluntas: International Journal of Voluntary and Nonprofit Organizations*, 5(3), 273–290.

Chang, C. F. & Tuckman, H. P. (1996). The goods produced by nonprofit organizations. *Public Finance Quarterly*, 24(1), 25–43.

Chikoto, G. L. & Neely, D. G. (2014). Building nonprofit financial capacity: The impact of revenue concentration and overhead costs. *Nonprofit and Voluntary Sector Quarterly*, 43(3), 570–588.

Clotfelter, C. T. (2002). The economics of giving. In J. Barry & B. Manno (Eds.), *Giving better, giving smarter* (pp. 31–55). Washington, DC: National Commission on Philanthropy and Civic Renewal.

Coupet, J. & Berrett, J. L. (2019). Toward a valid approach to nonprofit efficiency management. *Nonprofit Management & Leadership*, 29(3), 299–320.

Cordes, J. & Sansing, R. (2007). Institutional philanthropy. In D. R. Young (Ed.), *Financing nonprofits: Putting theory into practice* (pp. 45–68). Lanham, MD: AltaMira Press.

Cordes, J. J., & Weisbrod, B. A. (1998). Differential taxation of nonprofits and the commercialization of nonprofit revenues. *Journal of Policy Analysis and Management*, 17(2), 195–214.

Core, J. E., Guay, W. R., & Verdi, R. S. (2006). Agency problems of excess endowment holdings in not-for-profit firms. *Journal of Accounting and Economics*, 41, 307–333.

Crumpler, H. & Grossman, P. J. (2008). An experimental test of warm glow giving. *Journal of Public Economics*, 92, 1011–1021.

Deep, A. & Frumkin, P. (2001). The foundation payout puzzle. Working Paper No. 9, June. The Hauser Center for Nonprofit Organizations, the Kennedy School of Government, Harvard University.

Deep, A. & Frumkin, P. (2006). The foundation payout puzzle. In W. Damon and S. Verducci (Eds.), *Taking philanthropy seriously* (pp. 189–204). Bloomington, IN: Indiana University Press.

Denison, D. V. (2009). Which nonprofit organizations borrow? *Public Budgeting and Finance*, 29(3), 110–123.

De Wit, A. & Bekkers, R. (2016). Government support and charitable donations: A meta-analysis of the crowding-out hypothesis. *Journal of Public Administration Research and Theory*, 27(2), 301–319.

Dokko, J. K. (2009). Does the NEA crowd out private charitable contributions to the arts? *National Tax Journal*, 62(1), 57–75.

Duquette, N. J. (2017). Spend or save? Nonprofits' use of donations and other revenues. *Nonprofit and Voluntary Sector Quarterly*, 46(6), 1142–1165.

Eckel, C. C. & Steinberg, R. (1993). Competition, performance, and public policy towards nonprofits. In D. R. Young & D. C. Hammack (Eds.), *Nonprofit organizations in a market economy* (pp. 57–81). San Francisco, CA: Jossey-Bass.

Eikenberry, A. M.. & Kluver, J. D. (2004). The marketization of the nonprofit sector: Civil society at risk? *Public Administration Review, 64*(2), 132–140.

Eldenburg, L. & Vines, C. C. (2004). Nonprofit classification decisions in response to a change in accounting rules. *Journal of Accounting and Public Policy, 23*(1), 1–22.

Ely, T. L. & Calabrese, T. D. (2016). Leveling the playing field: The taxpayer relief act of 1997 and tax-exempt borrowing by nonprofit colleges and universities. *National Tax Journal, 69*(2), 387–411.

Ely, T. L. & Calabrese, T. D. (2017). Public borrowing for private organizations: Costs and structure of tax-exempt debt through conduit issuers. *Public Budgeting and Finance, 37*(1), 3–25.

Fernandez, K. M. & Hager, M. A. (2014). Public and private dimensions of grantmaking foundations. *Public Administration Quarterly, 38*(3), 405–439.

FASB (Financial Accounting Standards Board) (1993). *Statement of financial accounting standards no. 116: Accounting for contributions received and contributions made.* Norwalk, CT: FAF.

Faulk, L., Pandey, S., Pandey, S. K., & Kennedy, K. S. (2019). Donors' responses to profit incentives in the social sector: The entrepreneurial orientation reward and the profit penalty. *Journal of Policy Analysis and Management, 39*(1), 218–242.

Finkler, S. A., Smith, D. L., & Calabrese, T. D. (2020). *Financial management for public, health, and not-for-profit organizations*, 6th edition. Thousand Oaks, CA: CQ Press.

Fischer, M., Gordon, T., & Kraut, M. (2002). An examination of differences between financial information provided in IRS forms 990 and audited financial statements of US private colleges and universities. *Academy of Accounting and Financial Studies Journal 6*(1), 88.

Fischer, R. L. & Richter, F. G. C. (2017). SROI in the pay for success context: Are they at odds? *Evaluation and Program Planning, 64*, 105–109.

Fischer, R. L., Wilsker, A., & Young D. R. (2010). Exploring the revenue mix of nonprofit organizations: Does it relate to publicness? *Nonprofit and Voluntary Sector Quarterly, 40*(4), 662–681.

Fisman, R. & Hubbard, R. G. (2005). Precautionary savings and the governance of nonprofit organizations. *Journal of Public Economics, 89*, 2231–2243.

Foster, W. & Bradach, J. (2005). Should nonprofits seek profits? *Harvard Business Review, 83*(2), 92–100.

Foster, W. & Fine, G. (2007). How nonprofits get really big. *Stanford Social Innovation Review, 5*(2), 46–55.

Freeman, R. (1979). The job market for college faculty. In D. Lewis & W. Becker, Jr. (Eds.), *Academic rewards in higher education* (pp. 63–103). New York: Ballinger.

Frumkin, P. & Keating, E. K. (2010). The price of doing good: Executive compensation in nonprofit organizations. *Policy and Society, 29*, 269–282.

Frumkin, P. & Keating, E. K. (2011). Diversification reconsidered: The risks and rewards of nonprofit revenue concentration. *Journal of Social Entrepreneurship*, *2*(2), 151–164.

Galaskiewicz, J. & Bielefeld, W. (1998). *Nonprofit organizations in an age of uncertainty: A study of organizational change.* New York: de Gruyter.

Garcia-Rodriguez, I. & Jegers, M. (2017). Capital structure of nongovernmental development organizations: First cross-country evidence. *Nonprofit Management & Leadership*, *28*(2), 175–194.

Garven, S. A., Hofmann, M. A., & McSwain, D. N. (2016). Playing the numbers game: Program ratio management in nonprofit organizations. *Nonprofit Management & Leadership*, *26*(4), 401–416.

Gentry, W. M. (2002). Debt, investment, and endowment accumulation: The case of not-for-profit hospitals. *Journal of Health Economics*, *21*, 845–872.

Gneezy, U., Keenan, E. A., & Gneezy, A. (2014). Avoiding overhead aversion in charity. *Science*, *346*, 632–635.

Gordon, T. P., Knock, C. L., & Neely, D. G. (2009). The role of rating agencies in the market for charitable contributions: An empirical test. *Journal of Accounting and Public Policy*, *28*, 469–484.

Greenlee, J. S. & Trussel, J. M. (2000). Predicting the financial vulnerability of charitable organizations. *Nonprofit Management & Leadership*, *11*(2), 199–210.

Gregory, A. G. & Howard, D. (2009). The nonprofit starvation cycle. *Stanford Social Innovation Review* (August), 49–53.

Gronberg, T. J., Luccasen III, A., Turocy, T. L., & Van Huyck, J. B. (2012). Are tax-financed contributions to a public good completely crowded-out? *Journal of Public Economics*, *96*(7–8), 596–603.

Grønbjerg, K. A. (1992). Nonprofit human service organizations funding strategies and patterns of adaptation. In Y. Hasenfeld (Ed.), *Human services as complex organizations* (pp. 73–97). Newbury Park, CA: Sage.

Grønbjerg, K. A. & Clerkin, R. M. (2005). Examining the landscape of Indiana's nonprofit sector: Does what you know depend on where you look? *Nonprofit and Voluntary Sector Quarterly*, *34*(2), 232–259.

Grønbjerg, K. A., Liu, H. K., & Pollak, T. H. (2010). Incorporated but not IRS-registered: Exploring the (dark) grey fringes of the nonprofit universe. *Nonprofit and Voluntary Sector Quarterly*, *39*(5), 925–945.

Gruber, J. & Hungerman, D. M. (2007). Faith-based charity and crowd-out during the great depression. *Journal of Public Economics*, *91*(5–6), 1043–1069.

Hager, M. A. (2001). Financial vulnerability among arts organizations: A test of the Tuckman-Chang measures. *Nonprofit and Voluntary Sector Quarterly*, *30*(2), 376–392.

Handy, F., Seto, S., Wakaruk, A., Mersey, B., Mejia, A., & Copeland, L. (2010). The discerning consumer: Is nonprofit status a factor? *Nonprofit and Voluntary Sector Quarterly*, *39*(5), 866–883.

Hansmann, H. (1980). The role of nonprofit enterprise. *Yale Law Journal, 89*(5), 835–901.

Hansmann, H. (1981). The rationale for exempting nonprofit organizations from corporate income taxation. *The Yale Law Journal, 91*(1), 54–100.

Hansmann, H. (1987). The effect of tax exemption and other factors on the market share of nonprofit versus for-profit firms. *National Tax Journal, 40*(1), 71–82.

Hansmann. H. (1990). Why do universities have endowments? *Journal of Legal Studies, 19*(1), 3–42.

Hansmann, H. (1996). The changing roles of public, private, and nonprofit enterprise in education, health care, and other human services. In V. Fuchs (Ed.), *Individuals and social responsibility: Child care, education, medical care, and long-term care in America* (pp. 245–275). Chicago: University of Chicago Press.

Heist, H. D. & Vance-McMullen, D. (2019). Understanding donor-advised funds: How grants flow during recessions. *Nonprofit and Voluntary Sector Quarterly, 48*(5), 1066–1093.

Heshmat, S. (1992). Estimating the cost of capital for nonprofit hospitals. *Journal of Health and Human Resources Administration, 14*(4), 465–473.

Heutel, G. & Zeckhauser, R. (2014a). The investment returns of nonprofit organizations, Part I: Tales from 990 forms. *Nonprofit Management & Leadership, 25*(1), 41–57.

Heutel, G. & Zeckhauser, R. (2014b). The investment returns of nonprofit organizations, Part II: The value of focused attention. *Nonprofit Management & Leadership, 25*(1), 59–75.

Hirth, R. A. (1999). Consumer information and competition between nonprofit and for-profit nursing homes. *Journal of Health Economics, 18*(2), 219–240.

Hodgkinson, V. A. & Weitzman, M. S. (2001). Overview: The state of the independent sector. In J. S. Ott (Ed.), *The nature of the nonprofit sector* (pp. 9–22). Boulder, CO: Westview Press.

Holtz-Eakin, D. & Smith, C. (2010). Responding in crisis: An early analysis of foundations' grantmaking during the economic crisis. Available at https://www .unitedphilforum.org/resources/responding-crisis-early-analysis-foundations -grantmaking-during-economic-crisis.

Hooke, J., Yook, K., & Chu, W. (2019). Top foundations' 10-year plunge into alternatives yields mixed results and high fees. *Nonprofit Management & Leadership, 29*(3), 449–460.

Horne, C. S. (2005). *Toward an understanding of the revenue of nonprofit organizations.* Atlanta: Georgia Institute of Technology (doctoral dissertation).

Horne, C. S., Johnson, J. L., & Van Slyke, D. M. (2005). Do charitable donors know enough—and care enough—about government subsidies to affect private giving to nonprofit organizations? *Nonprofit and Voluntary Sector Quarterly, 34*(1), 136–149.

Hughes, P. N. & Luksetich, W. A. (1999). The relationship among funding sources for art and history museums. *Nonprofit Management & Leadership, 10*(1), 21–37.

Hung, C. & Hager, M. (2019). The impact of revenue diversification on nonprofit financial health: A meta-analysis. *Nonprofit and Voluntary Sector Quarterly, 48*(1), 5–27.

Hungerman, D. M. (2005). Are church and state substitutes? Evidence from the 1996 welfare reform. *Journal of Public Economics, 89*(11–12), 2245–2267.

Jacobs, P. & Wilder, R. P. (1984). Pricing behavior of non-profit agencies: The case of blood products. *Journal of Health Economics, 3*(1), 49–61.

Jacobs, F. A. & Marudas, N. P. (2009). The combined effect of donation price and administrative inefficiency on donations to US nonprofit organizations. *Financial Accountability & Management, 25*(1), 33–53.

James, E. (1983). How nonprofits grow: A model. *Journal of Policy Analysis and Management, 2*, 350–366.

James, E. (1986). Comment. In S. Rose-Ackerman (Ed.), *The economics of nonprofit institutions: Studies in structure and policy* (pp. 154–158). New York: Oxford University Press.

James, E. & Young, D. R. (2007). Fee income and commercial ventures. In D. R. Young (Ed.), *Financing nonprofits: Putting theory into practice* (pp. 93–119). Lanham, MD: AltaMira Press.

James, R. N. (2018). Cash is not king for fund-raising: Gifts of noncash assets predict current and future contributions growth. *Nonprofit Management & Leadership, 29*(2), 159–179.

Jegers, M. (1997). Portfolio theory and nonprofit financial stability: A comment and extension. *Nonprofit and Voluntary Sector Quarterly, 26*(1), 65–72.

Jegers, M. (2003). The sustainable growth rate of non-profit organisations: The effects of efficiency, profitability, and capital structure. *Financial Accountability & Management, 19*(4), 309–313.

Jegers, M. (2018). Capital structure. In B. A. Seaman & D. R. Young (Eds.), *Handbook of research on nonprofit economics and management* (pp. 87–96). Northampton, MA: Edward Elgar.

Jegers, M. & Verschueren, I. (2006). On the capital structure of non-profit organisations: An empirical study for Californian organisations. *Financial Accountability & Management, 22*(4), 309–328.

Jones, C. L. & Roberts, A. A. (2006). Management of financial information in charitable organizations. *The Accounting Review, 81*(1), 159–178.

Karlan, D. & List, J. (2007). Does price matter in charitable giving? Evidence from a large-scale natural field experiment. *American Economic Review, 97*(5), 1174–1193.

Kearns, K. (2007). Income portfolio. In D. R. Young (Ed.), *Financing nonprofits: Putting theory into practice* (pp. 291–314). Lanham, MD: AltaMira Press.

Keating, E. K., Parsons, L. M., & Roberts, A. A. (2008). Misreporting fundraising: How do nonprofit organizations account for telemarketing campaigns? *The Accounting Review, 83*(2), 417–446.

Kerlin, J. A. & Pollak, T. H. (2011). Nonprofit commercial revenue: A replacement for declining government grants and private contributions? *The American Review of Public Administration, 41*(6), 686–704.

Khanna, J., Posnett, J., & Sandler, T. (1995). Charity donations in the UK: New evidence based on panel data. *Journal of Public Economics, 56,* 257–272.

Khanna, J. & Sandler, T. (2000). Partners in giving: The crowding-in effects of UK government grants. *European Economic Review, 44,* 1543–1556.

Khumawala, S. B., Parsons, L. M., & Gordon, T. P. (2005). Assessing the quality of not-for-profit efficiency ratios: Do donors use joint cost allocation disclosures? *Journal of Accounting, Auditing, & Finance, 20*(3), 287–309.

Ki, E.-J. & Oh, J. (2018). Determinants of donation amount in nonprofit membership associations. *International Journal of Nonprofit Voluntary Sector Marketing, 23*(3), e1609.

Kim, M. & Van Ryzin, G. G. (2014). Impact of government funding on donations to arts organizations: A survey experiment. *Nonprofit and Voluntary Sector Quarterly, 43*(5), 910–925.

Kingma, B. R. (1993). Portfolio theory and nonprofit financial stability. *Nonprofit and Voluntary Sector Quarterly, 22*(2), 105–119.

Kingma, B. R. (1995). Do profits "crowd out" donations, or vice versa? The impact of revenues from sales on donations to local chapters of the American red cross. *Nonprofit Management & Leadership, 6*(1), 21–38.

Kocher, C. (2007). Hospital capital budgeting practices and their relation to key hospital characteristics: A survey of US manager practices. *Journal of Global Business Issues, 1*(2), 21.

Konrath, S. & Handy, F. (2018). The development and validation of the motives to donate scale. *Nonprofit and Voluntary Sector Quarterly, 47*(2), 347–375.

Krasteva, S. & Yildirim, H. (2013). (Un)Informed charitable giving. *Journal of Public Economics, 106,* 14–26.

Krasteva, S. & Yildirim, H. (2016). Information, competition, and the quality of charities. *Journal of Public Economics, 144,* 64–77.

Krishnan, R., Yetman, M. H., & Yetman, R. J. (2006). Expense misreporting in nonprofit organizations. *The Accounting Review, 81*(2), 399–420.

Krishnan, R. & Yetman, M. H. (2011). Institutional drivers of reporting decisions in nonprofit hospitals. *Journal of Accounting Research, 49*(4), 1001–1039.

Landry, C. E., Lange, A., List, J. A., Price, M. K., & Rupp, N. G. (2010). Is a donor in hand better than two in the bush? Evidence from a natural field experiment. *American Economic Review, 100*(3), 958–983.

Lecy, J. D. & Searing, E. A. (2015). Anatomy of the nonprofit starvation cycle: An analysis of falling overhead ratios in the nonprofit sector. *Nonprofit and Voluntary Sector Quarterly, 44*(3), 539–563.

Lecy, J. (2019). Open data for nonprofit research. Available at: https://lecy.github.io /Open-Data-for-Nonprofit-Research/.

Lee, K. (2006). Voluntary provision of public goods and administrative costs. *Public Finance Review, 34*(2), 195–211.

Lee, S. & Woroncowicz, J. (2019). Nonprofit cash holdings and spending: The missing role of government funding. *Nonprofit Management & Leadership, 29*(3), 321–340.

Li, H. & McDougle, L. (2017). Information source reliance and charitable giving decisions. *Nonprofit Management & Leadership, 27*(4), 549–560.

Lu, J. (2016). The philanthropic consequence of government grants to nonprofit organizations: A meta-analysis. *Nonprofit Management & Leadership, 26*(4), 381–400.

Markowitz, H. (1952). Portfolio selection. *Journal of Finance, 7*(1), 77–91.

Marudas, N. P. (2004). Effects of nonprofit organization wealth and efficiency on private donations to large nonprofit organizations. *Research in Governmental and Nonprofit Accounting, 11*, 71–92.

Marudas, N. P. (2015). An improved model of effects of accounting measures of inefficiency on donations. *Journal of Finance and Accountancy, 21*, 1–15.

Mayer, W. J., Wang, H. Egginton, J. F., & Flint, H. S. (2014). The impact of revenue diversification on expected revenue and volatility for nonprofit organizations. *Nonprofit and Voluntary Sector Quarterly, 43*(2), 374–392.

Mayer, L. H. (2016). The rising of the states in nonprofit oversight. *Nonprofit Quarterly* (August 11). Available at: https://nonprofitquarterly.org/2016/08/11/rising-states-non profit-oversight/.

McDougle, L. (2014). Understanding public awareness of nonprofit organizations: Exploring the awareness—confidence relationship. *International Journal of Nonprofit and Voluntary Sector Marketing, 19*(3), 187–199.

McKeever, B. S., Dietz, N. E., & Fyffe, S. D. (2016). *The nonprofit almanac: The essential facts and figures for managers, researchers, and volunteers*, 9th edition. Washington, DC: Urban Institute Press.

McKeever, B. S. (2018). *The nonprofit sector in brief 2018: Public charities, giving, and volunteering*. Urban Institute. Available at: https://nccs.urban.org/publication /nonprofit-sector-brief-2018#the-nonprofit-sector-in-brief-2018-public-charites -giving-and-volunteering.

Meier, S. & Frey, B. S. (2004). Matching donations: Subsidizing charitable giving in a field experiment. Zurich IEER Working Paper No. 181 (February). Available at: https://ssrn.com/abstract=508862 or http://dx.doi.org/10.2139/ssrn.508862.

Milofsky, C. & Blades, S. D. (1991). Issues of accountability in health charities: A case study of accountability problems among nonprofit organizations. *Nonprofit and Voluntary Sector Quarterly, 20*(4), 371–393.

Mitchell, G. E. (2017). Fiscal leanness and fiscal responsiveness: Exploring the normative limits of strategic nonprofit financial management. *Administration & Society*, *49*(9), 1272–1296.

Mitchell, G. E. & Calabrese, T. D. (2018). Proverbs of nonprofit financial management. *The American Review of Public Administration*, *49*(6), 649–661.

Moleskis, M., Alegre, I., & Canela, M. A. (2019). Crowdfunding entrepreneurial or humanitarian needs? The influence of signals and biases on decisions. *Nonprofit and Voluntary Sector Quarterly*, *48*(3), 552–571.

Newhouse, J. (1970). Toward a theory of nonprofit institutions: An economic model of a hospital. *American Economic Review*, *60*(1), 64–74.

Newman, G. E., Shniderman, A., Cain, D. M., & Sevel, K. (2019). Do the ends justify the means? The relative focus on overhead versus outcomes in charitable fundraising. *Nonprofit and Voluntary Sector Quarterly*, *48*(1), 71–90.

Nikolova, M. (2015). Government funding of private voluntary organizations: Is there a crowding-out effect? *Nonprofit and Voluntary Sector Quarterly*, *44*(3), 487–509.

Niskanen, J. (1971). *Bureaucracy and representative government*. London: Routledge.

Nonprofit Finance Fund (2018). State of the nonprofit sector survey, 2018. Available at: https://nff.org/sites/default/files/paragraphs/file/download/341454_NFF_Survey_R1_Proof.pdf.

Null, C. (2011). Warm glow, information, and inefficient charitable giving. *Journal of Public Economics*, *95*, 455–456.

Okten, C. & Weisbrod, B. A. (2000). Determinants of donations in private nonprofit markets. *Journal of Public Economics*, *75*, 255–272.

Olen, H. (2017). Is the new way to give a better way to give? Donor-advised funds are gaining popularity, but charities may be losing out. *The Atlantic* (December 13). Available at: https://www.theatlantic.com/business/archive/2017/12/donor-advised-funds-deduction-charity/548324/.

Olson, M. (1965). *The logic of collective action*. Cambridge, MA: Harvard University Press.

Omer, T. C. & Yetman, R. J. (2003). Near-zero taxable income reporting by nonprofit organizations. *Journal of the American Tax Association*, *25*(2), 19–34.

Oster, S. M. (1995). *Strategic management for nonprofit organizations: Theory and cases*. New York: Oxford University Press.

Pandey, S., Cordes, J. J., Pandey, S. K., & Winfrey, W. F. (2018). Use of social impact bonds to address social problems: Understanding contractual risks and transaction costs. *Nonprofit Management & Leadership*, *28*(4), 511–528.

Pauly, M. & Redisch, M. (1973). The not-for-profit hospital as a physicians' cooperative. *The American Economic Review*, *63*(1), 87–99.

Payne, A. A. (2001). Measuring the effect of federal research funding on private donations at research universities: Is federal research funding more than a substitute for
private donations? *International Tax and Public Finance, 8*(5–6), 731–751.

Powell, W. W. & Owen-Smith, J. (1998). Universities as creators and retailers of intellec-
tual property: Life-sciences research and commercial development. In B. A. Weisbrod
(Ed.), *To profit or not to profit: The commercial transformation of the nonprofit sector*
(pp. 169–193). New York: Cambridge University Press.

Preston, A. E. (1988). The nonprofit firm: A potential solution to inherent market failures. *Economic Inquiry, 26,* 493–506.

Qu, H. (2016). *Two essays on nonprofit finance.* Indianapolis: Indiana University (doctoral dissertation).

Qu, H. & Daniel, J. L. (2019). Is "overhead" a tainted word? A survey experiment
exploring framing effects of nonprofit overhead information on donor decision.
Paper presented at the 6th annual Science of Philanthropy Initiative conference,
September 19, Chicago, IL.

Qu, H, Steinberg, R., & Burger, R. (2019). Abiding by the law? Using Benford's law to
examine the accuracy of nonprofit financial reports. *Nonprofit and Voluntary Sector
Quarterly.* Available at: https://doi.org/10.1177/0899764019881510.

Reiser, D. B. & Dean, S. A. (2013). Hunting stag with fly paper: A hybrid financial instrument for social enterprise. *Boston College Law Review, 54*(4), 1495–1544.

Reiter, K. L., Smith, D. G., Wheeler, J. R. C., & Riverson, H. L. (2000). Capital investment
strategies in health care systems. *Journal of Health Care Finance, 26*(4), 31–41.

Renz, L. (2012). Understanding and benchmarking foundation payout. The Foundation
Center. Available at: http://foundationcenter.org/gainknowledge/research/pdf/pay
out2012.pdf.

Rondeau, D. & List, J. A. (2008). Matching and challenge gifts to charity: Evidence from
laboratory and natural field experiments. *Experimental economics, 11*(3), 253–267.

Rose-Ackerman, S. (1986). Do government grants to charity reduce private donations?
In S. Rose-Ackerman (Ed.), *The economics of nonprofit institutions: Studies in structure and policy* (pp. 313–329). New York: Oxford University Press.

Salamon, L. (1997). *Holding the center: America's nonprofit sector at a crossroads.* New
York: Nathan Cummings Foundation.

Salamon, L. M., Sokolowski, S. W., & Geller, S. L. (2012). Holding the fort: Nonprofit
employment during a decade of turmoil. Johns Hopkins University, Center for Civil
Society Studies. Nonprofit Economic Data Bulletin no. 39.

Salamon, L. M., Sokolowski, S. W., & Haddock, M. A. (2011). Measuring the economic
value of volunteer work globally: Concepts, estimates, and a roadmap to the future.
Annals of Public and Cooperative Economics, 82(3), 217–252.

Salamon, L. M., Sokolowski, S. W., Haddock, M. A., & Tice, H. S. (2013). The state of global civil society and volunteering. Johns Hopkins University, Center for Civil Society Studies. Comparative Nonprofit Sector Working Paper no. 49.

Sansing, R. (2010). Distribution policies of private foundations. In B. A. Seaman & D. R. Young (Eds.), *Handbook of research on nonprofit economics and management* (pp. 42–58). Northampton, MA: Edward Elgar.

Sansing, R. & Yetman, R. (2006). Governing private foundations using the tax law. *Journal of Accounting and Economics, 41*, 363–384.

Saxton, G. D., Oh, O., & Kishore, R. (2013). Rules of crowdsourcing: Models, issues, and systems of control. *Information Systems Management, 30*(1), 2–20.

Scanlon, W. J. (1980). A theory of the nursing home market. *Inquiry, 7*, 25–41.

Schiff, J. & Weisbrod, B. A. (1991). Competition between for-profit and nonprofit organizations in commercial activities. *Annals of Public and Cooperative Economics, 62*, 619–640.

Schlesinger, M., Mitchell, S., & Gray, B. (2004). Restoring public legitimacy to the nonprofit sector: A survey experiment using descriptions of nonprofit ownership. *Nonprofit and Voluntary Sector Quarterly, 33*, 673–710.

Schubert, P. & Boenigk, S. (2019). The nonprofit starvation cycle: Empirical evidence from a German context. *Nonprofit and Voluntary Sector Quarterly, 48*(3), 467–491.

Seaman, B. A. (2006). Empirical studies of demand for the performing arts. In V. A. Ginsburgh & D. Throsby (Eds.), *Handbook of the economics of art and culture* (pp. 415–472), Amsterdam, the Netherlands: North-Holland.

Segal, L. M. & Weisbrod, B. A. (1997). Interdependence of commercial and donative revenues. Institute for Policy Research at Northwestern University, IPR Working Paper No. 97–27.

Sloan, F. A. (1998). Commercialism in nonprofit hospitals. *Journal of Policy Analysis and Management, 17*(2), 234–252.

Sloan, F. A., Valvona, J., Hassan, M., & Morrisey, M. A. (1988). Cost of capital to the hospital sector. *Journal of Health Economics, 7*(1), 25–45.

Sloan, M. F., Charles, C., & Kim, M. (2016). Nonprofit leader perceptions of operating reserves and their substitutes. *Nonprofit Management & Leadership, 26*(4), 417–433.

Smith, D. H. (1997). The rest of the nonprofit sector: Grassroots associations as the dark matter ignored in prevailing "flat earth" maps of the sector. *Nonprofit and Voluntary Sector Quarterly, 26*(2), 114–131.

Smith, D. H. (2000). *Grassroots associations.* Thousand Oaks, CA: Sage.

Smith, D. H. (2014). The current state of civil society and volunteering in the world, the USA, and China. *China Nonprofit Review, 6*(1), 137–150.

Smith, D. H. (2015). Voluntary associations, sociology of. In J. D. Wright (Ed.), *International encyclopedia of the social & behavioral sciences*, 2nd edition, vol. 25 (pp. 252–260). Oxford: Elsevier.

Smith, D. H. (2017). Differences between nonprofit agencies and membership associations. In A. Farazmand (Ed.), *Global encyclopedia of public administration, public policy, and governance* (pp. 1404–1412). New York: Springer.

Steinberg, R. (1986a). The revealed objective functions of nonprofit firms. *The RAND Journal of Economics*, 17(4), 508–526.

Steinberg, R. (1986b). Should donors care about fundraising? In S. Rose-Ackerman (Ed.), *The economics of nonprofit institutions: Studies in structure and policy* (pp. 347–364). New York: Oxford University Press.

Steinberg, R. (1987). Voluntary donations and public expenditures in a federalist system. *American Economic Review*, 77(1), 24–36.

Steinberg, R. (1991). Does government spending crowd out donations? Interpreting the evidence. *Annals of Public and Cooperative Economics*, 62(4), 591–612.

Steinberg, R. (2006). Economic theories of nonprofit organizations. In W. W. Powell & R. Steinberg (Eds.), *The nonprofit sector: A research handbook*, 2nd edition (pp. 117–139). New Haven, CT: Yale University Press.

Steinberg, R. (2007). Membership income. In D. R. Young (Ed.), *Financing nonprofits: Putting theory into practice* (pp. 121–155). Lanham, MD: AltaMira Press.

Steinberg, R. (2015). What should social finance invest in and with whom? In A. Nicholls, R. Paton, & J. Emerson (Eds.), *Social finance* (pp. 64–95). Oxford: Oxford University Press.

Steinberg, R. & Galle, B. (2018). A law and economics perspective on nonprofit organizations. In M. Harding (Ed.), *Research handbook on not-for-profit law* (pp. 16–47). Northampton, MA: Edward Elgar.

Steinberg, R. & Gray, B. H. (1993). The role of nonprofit enterprise in 1993: Hansmann revisited. *Nonprofit and Voluntary Sector Quarterly*, 22(4), 297–316.

Steinberg, R. & Morris, D. (2010). Ratio discrimination in charity fundraising: The inappropriate use of cost ratios has harmful side-effects. *Voluntary Sector Review*, 1(1), 77–95.

Steinberg, R. & Weisbrod, B. A. (1998). Pricing and rationing by nonprofit organizations with distributional objectives. In B. A. Weisbrod (Ed.), *To profit or not to profit: The commercial transformation of the nonprofit sector* (pp. 64–82). New York: Cambridge University Press.

Strom, S. (2002). Nonprofit groups reach for profits on the side. *New York Times* (March 17).

Tevel, E., Katz, H., & Brock, D. M. (2015). Nonprofit financial vulnerability: Testing competing models, recommended improvements, and implications. *Voluntas*, 26, 2500–2516.

Tinkelman, D. (1998). Differences in sensitivity of financial statement users to joint cost allocations: The case of nonprofit organizations. *Journal of Accounting, Auditing & Finance, 13*, 377–393.

Tinkelman, D. (1999). Factors affecting the relation between donations to not-for-profit organizations and an efficiency ratio. *Research in Governmental and Nonprofit Accounting, 10*, 135–161.

Tinkelman, D. (2006). The decision-usefulness of nonprofit fundraising ratios: Some contrary evidence. *Journal of Accounting, Auditing, & Finance, 21*, 441–462.

Tinkelman, D. & Mankaney, K. (2007). When is administrative efficiency associated with charitable donations? *Nonprofit and Voluntary Sector Quarterly, 36*, 41–64.

Tinkelman, D. & Neely, D. G. (2018). Revenue interactions: Crowding out, crowding in, or neither? In B. A. Seaman & D. R. Young (Eds.), *Handbook of research on nonprofit economics and management*. Northampton, MA: Edward Elgar.

Tschirhart, M. (2006). Nonprofit membership associations. In W. W. Powell & R. Steinberg (Eds.), *The nonprofit sector: A research handbook*, 2nd edition (pp. 523–541). New Haven, CT: Yale University Press.

Trussel, J. M. (2002). Revisiting the prediction of financial vulnerability. *Nonprofit Management & Leadership, 13*, 17–31.

Trussel J. M. & Greenlee, J. S. (2004). A financial rating system for non-profit organizations. *Research in Government and Nonprofit Accounting, 11*, 105–128.

Tuckman, H. P. (1993). How and why nonprofit organizations obtain capital. In D. C. Hammack & D. R. Young (Eds.), *Nonprofit organizations in a market economy* (pp. 203–252). San Francisco, CA: Jossey-Bass.

Tuckman, H. P. & Chang, C. F. (1991). A methodology for measuring the financial vulnerability of charitable nonprofit organizations. *Nonprofit and Voluntary Sector Quarterly, 20*(4), 445–460.

Tuckman, H. P. & Chang, C. F. (1992). Nonprofit equity: A behavioral model and its policy implications. *Journal of Policy Analysis and Management, 11*(1), 76–87.

Tuckman, H. P. & Chang, C. F. (2006). Commercial activity, technological change, and nonprofit mission. In W. W. Powell & R. Steinberg (Eds.), *The nonprofit sector: A research handbook*, 2nd edition (pp. 629–644). New Haven, CT: Yale University Press.

Tullock, G. (1966). Information without profit. *Public choice, 1*(1), 141–159.

Vesterlund, L. (2006). Why do people give? In W. W. Powell & R. Steinberg (Eds.), *The nonprofit sector: A research handbook*, 2nd edition (pp. 168–190). New Haven, CT: Yale University Press.

Vesterlund, L. (2016). Using experimental methods to understand why and how we give to charity. In J. H. Kagel & A. E. Roth (Eds.), *Handbook of experimental economics*, vol. 2 (pp. 91–151). Princeton, NJ, and Oxford: Princeton University Press.

Wedig, G. J., Hassan, M., & Morrisey, M. A. (1996). Tax-exempt debt and the capital structure of nonprofit organizations: An application to hospitals. *The Journal of Finance*, *51*(4), 1247–1283.

Wedig, G., Sloan, F. A., Hassan, M., & Morrisey, M. A. (1988). Capital structure, ownership, and capital payment policy: The case of hospitals. *The Journal of Finance*, *43*(1), 21–40.

Weisbrod, B. A. (1975). Toward a theory of the voluntary nonprofit sector in a three-sector economy. In E. S. Phelps (Ed.), *Altruism, morality, and economic theory* (pp. 171–195). New York: Russell Sage Foundation.

Weisbrod, B. A. (1988). *The nonprofit economy*. Cambridge, MA: Harvard University Press.

Weisbrod, B. A. (1998). The nonprofit mission and its financing: Growing links between nonprofits and the rest of the economy. In B. A. Weisbrod (Ed.), *To profit or not to profit: The commercial transformation of the nonprofit sector* (pp. 1–22). New York: Cambridge University Press.

Weisbrod, B. A. & Schlesinger, M. (1986). Public, private nonprofit ownership and the response to asymmetric information: The case of nursing homes. In S. Rose-Ackerman (Ed.), *The economics of nonprofit institutions* (pp 133–151). New York: Oxford University Press.

Wicker, P. & Breuer, C. (2014). Examining the financial condition of sport governing bodies: The effects of revenue diversification and organizational success factors. *Voluntas: International Journal of Voluntary and Nonprofit Organizations*, *25*(4), 929–948.

Wilsker, A. L. & Young, D. R. (2010). How does program composition affect the revenues of nonprofit organizations? Investigating a benefits theory of nonprofit finance. *Public Finance Review*, *38*(2), 193–216.

Wing, K. & Hager, M. A. (2004). *Getting what we pay for: Low overhead limits nonprofit effectiveness*. Washington, DC: Urban Institute.

Wing, K., Gordon, T., Hager, M., Pollak, T., & Rooney, P. (2006). Functional expense reporting for nonprofits: The accounting profession's next scandal. *The CPA Journal*, August, 14–18.

Wong, C., Chua, V. C., & Vasoo, S. (1998). Contributions to charitable organizations in a developing country: The case of Singapore. *International Journal of Social Economics*, *25*(1), 25–42.

Yetman, M. H. & Yetman, R. J. (2003). The effect of nonprofits' taxable activities on the supply of private donations. *National Tax Journal*, *56*(1), 243–258.

Yetman, M. H. & Yetman, R. J. (2012). Do donors discount low-quality accounting information? *The Accounting Review*, 88(3), 1041–1067.

Young, D. R. (1981). Entrepreneurship and the behavior of nonprofit organizations: Elements of a theory. In M. White (Ed.), *Nonprofit firms in a three-sector economy* (pp. 135–162). Washington, DC: Urban Institute.

Young, D. R. (1998). Commercialism in nonprofit social service associations: Its character, significance, and rationale. *Journal of Policy Analysis and Management, 17*(2), 278–297.

Young, D. R. (2007). Toward a normative theory of nonprofit finance. In D. R. Young (Ed.), *Financing nonprofits: Putting theory into practice* (pp. 339–372). Lanham, MD: AltaMira Press.

Young, D. R. (2017). *Financing nonprofit and other social enterprises: A benefits approach.* Northampton, MA: Edward Elgar Publishing, Inc.

Young, D. R. & Lecy, J. D. (2014). Defining the universe of social enterprise: Competing metaphors. *Voluntas: International Journal of Voluntary and Nonprofit Organizations, 25,* 1307–1332.

Young, D. R. & Longhofer, W. (2016). Designing the zoo. In D. R. Young, E. A. Searing, & C. V. Brewer (Eds.), *The social enterprise zoo: A guide for perplexed scholars, entrepreneurs, philanthropists, leaders, investors, and policymakers.* (pp. 15–32). Northampton, MA: Edward Elgar.

Young, D. R. & Steinberg, R. (1995). *Economics for nonprofit managers.* New York: Foundation Center.

Young, D. R., Steinberg, R., Emanuele, R., & Simmons, W. O. (2019). *Economics for nonprofit managers and social entrepreneurs.* Northampton, MA: Edward Elgar.

Zhao, J. & Lu, J. (2019). The crowding-out effect within government funding: Implications for within-source diversification. *Nonprofit Management & Leadership, 29*(4), 611–622.

Zietlow, J. T. (1989). Capital and operating budgeting practices in pure nonprofit organizations. *Financial Accountability & Management, 5*(4), 219–232.

Printed in the United States
By Bookmasters